TO HELP YOU THROUGH THE HURTING

TO HELP YOU THROUGH THE HURTING

A Marjorie Holmes Treasury

Phoenix Press

WALKER AND COMPANY
New York

Large Print Edition published by
arrangement with Doubleday & Co., Inc.

Biblical quotes are from the King James and Revised Standard versions.

Grateful acknowledgment is made to the following for permission to reprint their copyrighted material:

"Come Home" from *You and I Yesterday* by Marjorie Holmes. Copyright © 1973 by Marjorie Holmes. By permission of William Morrow & Company

"Believe and Receive" originally "The Choice"; "To Sing So That Others May Hear"; "God Only Knows"; "The Suffering Few of Us Escape"; "If It Can Teach Us to Forgive"; "The Crosses"; "Cut Back the Vines"; "Persecution"; "God's Answer to Evil"; "For Every Cross I've Carried"; "Gone Where?"; "Dad's Roses"; "Mother's Bible"; "Face to Face"; "Promises to Keep"; "So Short, but Oh So Sweet"; "The Procession"; and "God Says, 'Get Up!'" from *How Can I Find You, God?* by Marjorie Holmes. Copyright © 1975 by Marjorie Holmes Mighell. Reprinted by permission of Doubleday & Company, Inc.

"This Hurt"; "He Was So Young"; "When Loneliness Is New"; "The Lonely Women"; "She Sits in Darkness"; "The Lovely Solitude"; "Psalm for Deliverance"; "The Radiant Company"; "The Adventure"; and "Myself" first appeared in *Who Am I, God?* by Marjorie Holmes. Copyright © 1970, 1971 by Marjorie Holmes Mighell. Published by Doubleday & Company, Inc.

"The Healing"; "Let Me Say 'Yes' to New Experiences"; "Don't Let Me Stop Growing" all first appeared in *Hold Me Up a Little Longer, Lord* by Marjorie Holmes. Copyright © 1971, 1972, 1973, 1974, 1975, 1976, 1977 by Marjorie Holmes Mighell. Published by Doubleday & Company, Inc.

"The Message"; "The Lesson of Loss"; "The New Dimension of Love"; and "When the Winds Cry I Hear You" from *I've Got to Talk to Somebody, God* by Marjorie Holmes. Copyright © 1968, 1969 by Marjorie Holmes Mighell. Reprinted by permission of Doubleday & Company, Inc. and Hodder & Stoughton Ltd.

"We'll Come" first appeared in *Love and Laughter* by Marjorie Holmes. Copyright © 1959, 1967 by Marjorie Holmes Mighell. Published by Doubleday & Company, Inc.

"At Christmas the Heart Goes Home" by Marjorie Holmes. Reprinted with permission from *Guideposts* magazine. Copyright © 1976 by Guideposts Associates, Inc., Carmel, New York, 10512. All rights reserved.

Printed in USA

Library of Congress Cataloging in Publication Data

Holmes, Marjorie, 1910–
    To help you through the hurting.

    1. Consolation.   2. Bereavement—Religious aspects—
Christianity.   3. Large type books.   I. Title.
[BV4905.2.H59   1985]   242'.4   85-10478
ISBN 0-8027-2508-2

First Large Print Edition, 1985
Walker & Company
720 Fifth Avenue
New York, New York 10019

For my husband,
Dr. George Peter Schmieler

Contents

Introduction

This book is a collection of things I have written about human hurting. Including that greatest hurt of all, losing someone you love.

I know how it feels. I have been there. And I have shared the terrible hurting of others.

We all need comfort. We all need hope. We all need to realize that "this too will pass." This is *not* the end for us. So long as there is life in our bodies, God wants us to get up and go on. When we do, he often has wonderful things in store for us.

It is my prayer that this little book will not only help you through the hurting . . . but help you to find them.

I

Pain

*Out of the depths have I cried
unto thee, O Lord.
Lord, hear my voice:
let thine ears be attentive
to the voice of my supplications.*
            Psalm 130:1–2

THIS HURT

Listen, Lord, please listen . . .

You will help me to bear this hurt. This seemingly intolerable pain.

You will help me not to cry out in agony. But you will be patient with me too; you will not ask me to be too brave inside.

This hurt, oh God, this hurt.

It is a shock, it dazes and numbs me. So that for a little while I can move blindly, almost insensate, about my duties.

Then it revives, it comes again in waves, rhythmic beatings that seem almost not to be borne. Yet I know that I must bear them, as a woman endures the pains of birth.

I am in labor, Lord. A terrible labor of the spirit. And it is infinitely worse than childbirth because right now I can see no deliverance. And I will have nothing to show for it.

Or—will I? Will I, Lord?

Surely I will have new strength in

5

compensation. *Surely somewhere inside me there will be some hard sustaining residue, some accretion of anguish like the mineral deposits from water, or rocks hardened out of a volcano's boiling lava.*

Perhaps this very pain is building a rock cliff within me that will stand stern against further assaults of pain and grief. And it will be both a protection and a base from which to start anew.

Thank you for this revelation. You who are truly the "rock of ages" will support me and help to build in me this other rock of strength.

BELIEVE AND RECEIVE

I must tackle the subject of suffering, God. I must wrestle with the problem of finding you and not letting go in spite of the awful injustices of your world, in spite of pain.

You know I don't understand it—I don't think many people do, no matter what they claim. I sometimes feel very stupid. Again

6

and again it is explained to me, the purpose and need of suffering. And I listen and nod and agree.

Then I see people who've lived lives of great goodness and sacrifice die sudden dreadful deaths; or trembling through long lonely living deaths in nursing homes. . . . I see the horrible ravages of famine and wars. . . . And the children—O dear God, the little children neglected, abused, raped. Or born crippled, mute, blind.

And my very soul rages, I don't BLAME you, but there is no sure heart-knowledge of mercy or justice within me. I can only accept the fact (and ask you to forgive me) that I can't accept some things.

 I can only trust to such sure heart-knowledge as I have: That suffering does not come from you. But it is not in vain. It DOES serve some purpose in the total scheme of things. And you expect us to take it. Take it without too much breast-beating and weeping and wailing, "Not fair!" TAKE it and MAKE it work for our own soul's growth.

I can't believe you deliberately send it for that reason, God. But since we are stuck with it (or you are stuck with it) you will help see us through it. You will help us overcome it, and emerge purer, finer, better because of it. Above all, closer to you.

In *personal* suffering we can find you. Know you as never before.

As for other people's suffering? The appalling injustices we are forced to witness and before which we feel so impotent? These I cannot and must not ignore. These I must do all that I can to assuage.

Yet I cannot and must not let them stand between me and my God. To do so would only add my own misery to the weight of human despair. I must have you, God, to sustain me. I must have your help if I am to know any happiness as a human being, and so be able to help anyone else.

My choice is this: "To doubt and do without," as someone has said. Or "to believe and receive." I believe, Lord, I believe. And even in times of trouble—yes, even more richly in times of trouble—I receive!

TO SING SO THAT OTHERS MAY HEAR

One of the best articles I've ever read on suffering was written by one of the two Hopes in my life, Hope Good; it appeared in the magazine *Orion*. In it she told of once having a rabbit whose cage was ripped apart by dogs one night and the pet torn to bits. She wept for days, asking, "How could a loving God have permitted such a catastrophe? Suddenly, like a revelation, I concluded that I was to this creature as God is to me, yet I was unable to assist when it needed me. Yes, God loves us with a deep compassion, even when He is unable to come to our aid."

She went on to say, "We must stop asking, Why did this happen to me? Instead, we must ask ourselves: How can I use it creatively? . . . There is no evil so terrible that it cannot, with God's help, be used . . . the challenge to make something of value replace a failure, defeat or disappointment is about the only way man has to answer the problem of suffering."

Another clipping, yellow with age. Written by former Senate chaplain Frederick Brown Harris in his column "Spires of the Spirit." He called this one "Dialing the Man Upstairs." "The object in dialing God is never to demand, 'Get me out of this,' but 'Save me from surrendering to this.' We haven't mastered the first lesson in the Primer of Life's meaning until we know that the chief end of man is not comfort, but character.... If character were the goal, rather than comfort, then a lot of things that otherwise seem to have no business here would make some sense."

To become not bitter—but better. To compensate. To turn the affliction into something fine. Artists always do this; a part of their genius is the ability to translate their sufferings into their greatest symphonies, sculpture, paintings, poems. But one needn't be a genius. "Out of the night that covers me, / Black as the Pit from pole to pole, / I thank whatever gods there may be / For my unconquerable soul," my mother used to quote from "Invictus." And every day, out of the dark night of suffering, shine forth unconquerable souls. With lights so vivid they brighten the way for others.

Following are two of the many I have known personally:

BARBIE

Born with a clot which caused the blood to back up, to rupture and hemorrhage in the esophagus and stomach. Years of intense pain and stress, hospitalizations, surgeries—one to remove her esophagus and a third of her upper stomach. A last-ditch life-saving effort, which left a hole in her neck for saliva to drain out, and another hole made directly into her stomach through the abdomen into which liquids could be fed. Agonizing, weakening bouts with hiccuping . . . yet this brave girl donned high-necked dresses, dated, went to school, held part-time jobs, sang in the choir—and wound up cheering those who came to cheer her!

During all this she was writing to her family and friends; remarkable letters which became a journal of courage and faith.

Listen to this, written at fifteen, after

11

hearing a moving sermon about total commitment:

I sat in the balcony in the "cry room" (for mothers with babies) where I could hear Pastor Bob but no one could hear me [hiccuping]. I sat up there half-drugged from my tranquilizers, angry, scared, and very discouraged. . . . Afterward, I went up to talk to him. He had told about a lady in his church who had tried to commit suicide before she'd found Christ and turned her life over to Him to control, and I wanted to know what he'd told HER. I told him I didn't understand why this had to happen to me again; and I asked him— if God is such a God of Love, then why is He doing this to me? We talked for a while, then prayed together, and I went home to do just what he told me to.

I went to my room and I prayed: "God, forgive my anger at You, and my discouragement. I know it's wrong, but I'm desperate, Lord. . . . Father, I give up fighting AGAINST having it—and fighting with You OVER it. If this is what You want for my life, even though I don't understand it, I accept it. So here is my life for

You to do with whatever you want to. God, I believe YOU'RE now in control. Thank You!"

Man, when you say that, look out—things are going to start to happen!

She fell asleep without help for the first time in weeks, she relates, and woke up hours later with the hiccups gone.

Now no one can tell me there is no God or that God is dead or that He doesn't love and watch over His children.

I KNOW I have a God, and that my God is alive, and that my God loves me!

Barbie's battle was far from over. At sixteen she was forced to write after unsuccessful surgery:

"Satan's cause is never more in danger than when a human no longer desiring, but still intending to do God's will, looks around him upon a universe from which every trace of Him seems to have vanished, and asks why he has been forsaken, and still obeys."

This quote from C. S. Lewis so perfectly depicts my situation as I lay in the Intensive Care Unit. . . . I was disappointed that the surgery had failed, terribly frustrated that I was sick AGAIN, that I was born this way with no hope of ever changing it, that I was missing out on school activities, most of all I was just TIRED of hurting so much!

Then the Lord stepped in and said, "Now wait a minute. What is the last thing you did in that operating room before you went to sleep?" I said, "Well, I committed my life completely into your hands and thanked you in advance for being my Sufficiency. . . ." "O.K. then," He said. "What are you getting so upset about? . . ."

She then prayed the famous Serenity Prayer:

God grant me the serenity to accept the things I cannot change, the courage to change the things I can, and the wisdom to know the difference.

And concluded:

I can't change the fact that I was born with

14

a birth defect, but I CAN change my attitude toward it.

Her high school picture smiles from the letter she wrote shortly before her eighteenth birthday. A radiantly beautiful dark-eyed girl, saying:

It has now been fifteen months since my esophagus had to be removed, and the doctors are still at a complete loss as to how to put me back together again. But in fulfilling His promise—"I can do all things through Christ who strengtheneth me"—it was made possible for me to combine my junior and senior years into one, and with the help of a wonderful tutor, to maintain a "B-plus" average, so I WILL walk down that aisle to receive my diploma with my class!

Barbie was almost nineteen when she wrote her final letter. Still intending to go to college, yet aware that the Lord might have other plans for her.

Oh, Pastor Luther, I do praise and thank Him from my innermost being. Because as one of the verses from your text Sunday says, "They should SEEK the Lord, if haply they might feel after Him and FIND Him, though He be NOT FAR FROM ANY ONE OF US. For in Him we live, and move, and have our being!" (See—I listened!!)

... John 11:4 says, "This sickness is not unto death, but for the glory of God ..." But I'm not afraid to die, because if that is His ministry for me, then I am willing. And He CAN use me in this way, in EVERY way. . . . I am totally, completely His, to do with as He chooses.

The entire story of Barbie Hertel is being told in a book written by her mother. . . . Meanwhile, a school library building is being named for her, and the impact of her gallantry, her faith in the face of suffering, can never be measured. . . .

ELIAS

A young Greek musician performing in a strange land. A slight limp, a long history of leg problems. Now—cancer, the doctors say. The limb must come off. . . . The night before the amputation he asks for his guitar. We bring it and he lies in bed tuning it lovingly. Then he begins to play and softly sing. Beautiful, heart-melting Grecian love songs. And it is so poignant and lovely the nurses begin to peer in. And other patients. They stand and listen, young and old. One a very old black man. And a young mother from her vigil in the children's wing.

Can she bring some children to hear him? she asks. Will he share his music with them? He says yes, of course, bring the children. And she comes leading them, three little girls who have had tracheotomies. Their throats are bandaged, none of them can speak. But they gaze at him with awed delight, these silent five- and six-year-olds. They keep time with their hands. And as the music quickens and he nods and smiles at them, one of them begins to dance around in her robe, her little slippers.

He leans toward them, his great dark eyes alight. "I play some songs you know, ha? You know 'Frère Jacques'?" They nod and he begins to sing, urging them to join in: "Frère *Jacques* . . . Frère *Jacques*—" And though they can't make a sound, their lips

17

move, miming the words. With his smile and his eyes he encourages them.

Then he moves into one that makes them bounce: "This old man, he played *one*, he played nick-nack on my drum. . . . With a *nick-nack*, paddy-whack, give a dog a bone, *this* old man came rolling home!" They are beating time, the tiny one in pigtails tries to dance, too, mute but joyfully they "sing."

A sassy little black nurse pops in, joins the fun, warbling in a high foolish falsetto before ordering, "Now hold still, Mr. Music Man, for your shot." Attention is focused on the doomed leg lying in its heavy white cast. The foot protrudes, and into it the needle goes. Elias takes up his guitar again, finishes the next tune with the brisk familiar rhythm—"Shave and a haircut, six bits!" The children laugh and the one with the huge blue eyes clicks her tongue to echo its beat. Then, thanking him, the young mother shepherds them away.

Lights are being lowered, the others have left, too. We turn to tell him good night, each gripping a hand on either side of the bed. We say a little prayer for him. When his eyes open they are wet, but he continues to smile. "Now don't you worry, I be okay."

The next time we see him the leg is gone. He is in great pain. But he touches the tiny cross around his neck and forms the words silently, like the children—"I'm okay. I'm okay."

GOD ONLY KNOWS

Common expressions have a way of packaging truths.

Consider: "God only knows."

How often we say this when we come up against something we can't explain. Usually something we object to, something of which we despair. "Why did this have to happen? . . . God knows!" Or "God only knows."

Slang, yes . . . but wait, isn't it maybe something more? Can this be the voice of the soul itself speaking? Handing over to God a mystery too much for us. Saying, in essence—*God* knows . . . God *does* know. . . . And only God.

The speaker may not even be a believer, merely someone resigning the matter to fate.

Yet the persistence of the soul's knowledge is there. . . . For we can't hope to understand all the secrets of the universe or the total nature of God or even of his complex creation, man.

We are so human. Faulty and finite. Boxed within certain physical limits, at least during our stay on earth. We can't fly in the air under our own power, or sustain ourselves under water unless we have aids. . . . And we have cleverly invented such aids; things we could not have imagined a few years ago we have now achieved. . . . Such progress! Yet how far are we able to progress in the matters of mind and spirit? How long will it take us to understand God?

Loving God and feeling his presence does not mean for a minute that we are his equals. . . . The maker of one single river . . . or the sun . . . or me! How can I hope to comprehend his mystery?

I just know that I am his child. And you are his child. And no matter what happens in this life or beyond it, he will not forsake us. . . . Meanwhile, when things occur that are beyond my feeble comprehension, things that test my faith, scald my spirit, rend my secret being, I can indeed cry out in sheer human dismay, resistant and yet resigned—yes, and reverent:

"God knows why. God only knows!"

While the still small voice of my deeper soul-knowledge whispers reassuringly: "Yes. God knows."

THE SUFFERING FEW OF US ESCAPE

You know what a coward I am about suffering, God. My own or other people's.

I would never have made a martyr; once they started to beat me or drag me to the lions I'm afraid I'd have recanted. If I were imprisoned and they tortured me for secrets, I don't think I could stand it—I'd tell!

And I am sickened before the spectacle of suffering, any physical suffering, of man or animal. (How can anyone be entertained by brutal acts? How can anyone cheer at the sight of any creature bruised, bleeding, struggling desperately to escape?)

21

It's hard for me even to READ *about suffering. If I am helpless to stop it, it seems witless to punish my own flesh and soul by drinking in the dread details. . . .*

No, no, I must flee from physical suffering.

Yet there is another kind of suffering few of us can flee. And that we cannot stop by a mere act of will: not by averting our eyes, running away, slamming the door.

The agony of love in all its variations.

Man and woman love. The many aspects of love between male and female . . . Anxiety about the one so close to us . . . Long separations . . . Conflicts, quarrels, doubts . . . Husband and wife who've forgotten how to talk to each other . . . Indifference . . . The bitter wounds of unfaithfulness . . . To be denied the person most deeply loved . . . The awful unfulfilled hungers of body and soul . . .

These our private crucifixions.

And children: O God, dear God, the multiple crucifixions we undergo for our children. Nailed to the cross again and again for their shortcomings. Or only waiting at the cross sometimes (which can be worse) forced to witness their suffering.

So I am no stranger to suffering. And I can't honestly call myself a coward before these emotional assaults. In some ways I feel brave before them. I have faced them before, most of them, and will face them again and survive. You give me the strength, you give me the courage.

You make me realize that anyone who drinks from the sweet cup of love must also swallow the gall. But love is worth it . . . ah, but it's worth it! And if you truly love, as Jesus taught, then the price we pay for love has even more value.

In suffering for love of others we are also suffering for love of you. This suffering I welcome, Lord.

IF IT CAN TEACH US TO FORGIVE

My heart broke for this daughter, so young to be suffering so much. The *if onlys* piled up . . . *If only* we could have talked them

23

out of the too-early marriage. *If only* we'd had the right answers or been able to help when the problems got bad . . .

But now the worst of it is over, and she emerges from the years of trial still young and calm and strong and—incredibly—even closer to God: "Mother, listen, just because we love God and he loves us doesn't mean we're not going to have *pain*. Pain is the price we pay on earth for loving someone. But the pain of love—that's the kind of pain that can make us realize the true nature of God.

"How could I turn my back on Jesus just because I have suffered over human love? I understand now how *he*, Jesus, feels. How he must suffer over loving us so much, when so many people don't know or love him."

She speaks of her marriage without regret; they both learned so much from each other. "And who knows what time will bring? Who knows the impact we have on other lives? Who knows what God can do, how much good he can build out of our mistakes? The fact that we could forgive each other for the pain we caused each other, isn't that what Jesus wants? Isn't that a

24

pretty big thing? Yes, of course it hurts, but even hurting isn't in vain if it can teach us to forgive."

THE CROSSES

Morning . . . a broad green Iowa pasture where the children and I used to hike . . . Crawl gingerly under the barbed-wire fence, then up the hill and on through the tall tossing grasses. Lurking among this growth are the lavender thistles, pronged and pert, like imps to be wary of. Birds spurt ahead— quails and blackbirds red-winged and gold. Meadow larks call from the fences. Everywhere the bird cries are ringing and chirring and caroling. How many there are—a bird Paradise.

The green-golding weeds and grasses have a gilded look in the morning sun. They wash and shine and make their own soft music. They bend toward the bank. The ground pitches toward this bank, and at its edge you look down upon the stream, broad and clear and sparkling, winding between

25

these escarpments. In the distance more fields, and the houses of the town Le Mars, and highways where cars and a few trucks race along. Yet here all is wide and vast, peaceful and free.

I walk along the bank and then down its side to be near the water, where there are glittering sandy beaches, and then thick muddy tracks where the cows have been. The mud is very black and rutted from their hooves; it squishes underfoot and sinks softly, and my sneakers turn black at the edge. I plod along until I reach the dry place and then consider climbing back. . . . And standing there wondering which is the least steep, I am aware of telephone poles that swing along the division between pasture and plowed cornfield. Poles standing slender and tall and spread-armed against the sky.

Or are they telephone poles? Utility poles probably, because they have a crosspiece, they make the form of the cross. And at the tip of each arm and at its crest is a small ornament that must have something to do with power. A glass insulator, maybe? Whatever it is, it adorns this cross—these gentle, graceful, stately crosses as they repeat themselves, at first large ... then smaller ... smaller ... dwindling to the eye against the sky.

For some reason I start up the steepest bank, and discover it isn't very steep, after all. Following a slightly zigzag course, I go bounding to the top ... and stand arrested once more by the sight of the crosses through which the silent power sings.

The image of the cross itself is enhanced. ... Is man driven, I wonder, to repeat this design in so many areas of his life? Or is it that the cross was and remains a plain, practical arrangement of timbers or anything else, to support death ... or life? In any case, here are these simple, lovely crosses against the blue morning country sky. And I am held by the sight.

The cross, symbol of sin and suffering— this beautiful geometrical design. And comfort and inspiration to so many ... Christ suffered for us and he took away our sins. But he couldn't spare us the suffering; not even he! Yet isn't the empty cross the symbol of suffering that is over and done with?

Of the man who died there and then walked free?

I understand now what my friend Hope Applebaum meant when she said once, "You have to suffer. You have to go through Gethsemane before you can rise." At the time I knew what she was saying, but it had no real significance. Now it seems as clear and clean as the country air.... All these crosses! They mark the landscape of our lives.

Even as I stand there looking at the utility poles I see that they have double arms. There are crosses piled upon crosses.... We often carry several crosses at a time. And yet each is gemmed with its little vital star of power. And the time eventually comes when that particular cross has served its purpose; the hour of suffering is over and the cross is empty. The man or woman walks free.

Now that I have become aware of crosses I see them wherever I am. Fashioning a child's kite, looking up at the mast of a sailing ship—always the central spire and the arms outspread. It is an image of balance and beauty, of both surrender and blessing.

And the crosses in all the windows of the

world! The shape of the cross that is made by the central lines of windowpanes. . . . Coming into an English village one night at sunset, the winding streets so narrow you could almost reach out from the bus and touch the cottages on either side . . . and each cottage window ablaze with the sun, as if to illuminate the black crosses that divide the glass.

It was like suddenly seeing a whole forest of small black crosses alight to welcome us. I said to my daughter, "Look, look!" And she, too, saw the phenomenon. Not only here but every place we went—on the streets of London, in the windows of loft or shop or pub, the cross as clearly defined, once you watch for it, as on the spires of cathedrals.

All those crosses, like a silent signal, inescapable, reassuring. Reminding us of the many trials people can endure and yet every day go cheerfully on . . .

But let's not get too poetic about crosses. They are beautiful from a distance, yes. During those times of life when we have put ours down (if only for a little rest); when we've grown enough to know the value, get perspective. . . . But when you're *carrying* one! (Or more.)

The thing to remember is this: We are not alone. Each of us has a cross to bear. The fact that we may not see another person's cross, often don't even suspect it, doesn't mean it isn't there. Hidden, so often bravely hidden behind a smile, a laugh, a proud carriage, a job superbly done—hidden behind locked doors—yet the cross is there. Again and again I have been staggered at the eventual revelations. Shocked to discover how many people had been going through their private crucifixions . . .

Crucifixions for others. Parents crucified for their children's mistakes. The husband or wife of an alcoholic crucified hour by hour. Not intentionally—few people deliberately set out to hurt those close to them—yet the inevitable Golgotha is there. So many, oh so many innocent victims! Nailed to the cross of our terrible concern for those we love, we bleed for them, and there is no freedom for our tormented spirits until they, too, are free.

Yet doesn't this, too, draw us closer to God? By sharing Christ's cup of suffering, don't we taste the true communion? And if we can love as he loved, forgive as he forgave, we, too, can be uplifted.

No personal crucifixion need ever be in vain.

THE HEALING

Thank you, Lord, that tonight my heart is light. Like something newly freed. For I have discovered how to heal it of an unexpected wound; one of those slight, seemingly small rebuffs or humiliations or blows that ought not to hurt so much, but for some of us who are unduly sensitive maybe, they do: A bawling out from the boss. A scolding from someone dear. A sharp word from a friend. Even rudeness from a stranger.

Such things can strike the sunshine from the day. The spirit winces, beats a quick retreat. We feel our wet eyes sting.

Then pride urges retaliation. Sometimes we want to turn on somebody else, as if to pass the pain along. Only now, Lord, I know the true way to relief is to cancel out the pain by doing something kind.

Thank you that today, still seething and suffering, I found myself seated on a bus beside a small shabby man. And I realized, as he stared fixedly out the window, that he was struggling not to cry. And my own little hurt seemed to shrink before the enormity of his. I knew I must speak to him—and did.

And he turned to me, Lord, and drew from his threadbare wallet a picture of a bright-eyed little girl six years old. "We lost her yesterday," he said. He was going now to pick out flowers. He wanted to talk about it. He was glad somebody cared. In our few blocks' ride across the city we shared it—his pride in her and his great loss.

And we touched upon the mystery of being born at all, of being parents, *of the brevity and beauty of life upon your earth.* And when we parted he was actually smiling. "You've made me feel so much better," he said.

"You've made me feel better too," I told him. For my own petty pain no longer mattered. It was as if some balance had been struck between that which is hurtful and that which is healing.

And perhaps that is all that really matters. That the good, the kind, the decent in this world can equal and even surpass the bad.

Thank you that I have learned this lesson, Lord. Next time it surely won't be so hard to overcome an unexpected hurt.

CUT BACK THE VINES

"Go cut back the grapes," I tell my son. "They're too thick, they've practically taken over the garage."

Naturally he has urgent business elsewhere; but after the usual argument he grabs the pruning shears and dashes outdoors. I hear him whacking away.

I look out later, and am aghast. The garage walls are naked. He has severed the lush growth clear back to the ground. "You've ruined them!" I accuse. "We'll never have grapes there again."

Wrong. The grapes came back the following year with an abundance never known

33

before; great purple clusters, fat and sweet, so heavy they bowed the trellis. It was just as Jesus said: "Every branch in me that beareth not fruit, he taketh away: and every branch that beareth fruit, he purgeth it, that it may bring forth more fruit" (John 15:2).

I thought of the ruthless slashing. The seeming waste. My scolding protests and my son's innocent bewilderment—he'd thought it was what I wanted. Our misunderstanding. The great fire we had to have even to dispose of the old branches . . . and now this! The newer, stronger, invigorated vines. The harvest so plentiful we carried basketsful to the neighbors.

"He purgeth it . . ." Pain and problems, the conflicts and disappointments, the defeats, the tragedies to which we all are subject—are they not purgings? I look back on my life sometimes in amazement before the memories of those terrible cuttings. Those times of trial by fire, it seemed. . . . Intolerable, intolerable. Rescue me, spare me! . . . Yet now I realize they were essential to my growth. How much hostility had to go in the process, how much self-pity, how much pride. A tangle of choking, life-impeding habits threatening to deny all that God meant me to be. I, too, had to be cut back, laid low.

And somehow, in the midst of it, I realized I could not go it alone, Lord. It was too much. I could not handle the weight of it, the people, the problems, the family, my job as a wife and mother, my fate as a woman in this demanding world, without support beyond my own.

Those words in John—all of them—must have been written for me: "Abide in me, and I in you. As the branch cannot bear fruit of itself, except it abide in the vine; no more can ye, except ye abide in me.

"I am the vine, ye are the branches: he that abideth in me, and I in him, the same bringeth forth much fruit: for without me ye can do nothing" (John 15:4–5).

It was like that. I saw that without you I could do nothing. You are the vine, not me. Weak and faulty as I was, I'd been trying to be the vine, holding up all the branches. I was just a branch and I had to be pruned, I had to be stripped if my roots were to be strengthened. Then only then could I bring forth much fruit!

PERSECUTION

It is a common paradox that persecution only intensifies faith. Strange. Why? Does God release some extra dimension of power when things get really rough?

Those early Christians, stoned, whipped, burned . . . what sustained them? What gave them the courage to suffer and die? But more, seeing their fate, what kept the rest of them from turning traitor? Instead, the very blood shed seemed to nourish the Christian soil, new converts sprang up.

What would have happened to Christianity without opposition? I wonder. Supposing the Romans and Greeks and unconverted Jews had said, "Okay, go ahead, don't mind us." Supposing they'd built churches instead of hiding out to worship in caves and homes? Would they have preached with such passion? Could they have drawn others to the cross if they hadn't been forced to carry their own—and to die on them? Supposing it had all been made easy. Would Christianity have become the living force it has been through the ages?

Would it even have survived?

In our own time—the persecutions in communist countries . . . the Soviet Union, East Germany, Albania, Czechoslovakia, Yugoslavia . . . people crowd into darkened homes. To share a single Bible, to pray and sing. Sometimes just to listen to someone who *remembers* the Bible. And when he comes, this Dutchman who can be known only as Brother Andrew, with the Bibles he has been able to smuggle across the border, carefully rationing them out—they weep for joy and risk arrest to have one in their possession. . . .

(My church is never locked. There are half a dozen churches within walking distance of my house. I have more versions of the Bible than I can count. What do they matter? Really *matter?* I can go to church or read a Bible anytime I want—so I put it off. . . . No, it isn't ease that intensifies faith, it is desperation and denial.)

God's Smuggler. Richard Wurmbrand's *Underground Saints.* And that other staggering book of Wurmbrand's, *In God's Underground.* . . . These modern martyrs—I read their stories of sacrifice,

37

imprisonment, torture, the incredible things they are still undergoing for God, and am ashamed. My own problems pale. I have never been persecuted. I have never suffered, at least not like that.

Could I if I had to, Lord?

This is not to say that you or I or God would willingly inflict such torment on anyone. But we must recognize that good can come of it. That there is no evil so terrible that good can't come of it. And sometimes a stark, bone-deep realization of how much God really means to us can come in no other way.

We turn to God, too, as individuals or en masse when all hope seems lost and there *is* no other way. (Why not *from* God when even he seems unable to deliver us from the tangible evil? Why *to*?)

Stalin's "planned and deliberate famine" intended to break the peasants' resistance to collectivization. . . . Malcolm Muggeridge describes the terrible toll in *Chronicles of Wasted Time*. And how he went to a

38

crowded church one morning in Kiev, after witnessing it.

Young and old, peasants and townsmen, parents and children . . . Never before or since have I participated in such worship; the sense conveyed of turning to God in great affliction was overpowering . . . for instance where the congregation say there is no help for them save from God. What intense feeling they put into those words! In their minds, I knew, as in mine, was a picture of those desolate abandoned villages, of the hunger and the hopelessness, of the cattle trucks being loaded with humans in the dawn light.

Where were they to turn for help? Not to the Kremlin and the Dictatorship of the Proletariat, certainly; nor to the forces of progress and democracy and enlightenment in the West. . . . Every possible human agency found wanting. So only God remained, and to God they turned with a passion, a dedication, a humility, impossible to convey. They took me with them; I felt closer to God then than I ever had before, or am likely to again.

Such reactions are intuitive, leading to truths too profound to question. They go back beyond time, back to Job and Lamentations and the hillsides where David sang his songs of worshipful desperation:

I cried unto the Lord with my voice, and he heard me out of his holy hill. Selah. I laid me down and slept; I awakened; for the Lord sustained me. I will not be afraid of ten thousands of people who have set themselves against me . . . (Psalm 3:4–6).

It is as if we are led by strong supernal forces. Driven by the soul's surest wisdom: This way, this way!

Come unto me, all ye that labour and are heavy laden, and I will give you rest (Matt. 11:28).

GOD'S ANSWER TO EVIL

Isn't the strength that is born of suffering God's answer to evil? God does not will the suffering, cannot or does not prevent it, cannot or does not always take it from us. But within each of us he has implanted a precious core of power mightier than the atom. Call it what you will, survival mechanism maybe, the stubborn will to overcome. But trigger it, arouse it, stir it with enough pain and despair and humiliation, enflame it, feed it with human blood, and look out. The explosion can rock the world.

It happened in a mass sense with our black people; and it happens in an individual sense every day. Jaws jutted, teeth bared, eyes flashing, human beings emerge from hell to declare: "Nothing is impossible to me now!"

Somewhere at this moment—on a hospital bed or in a prison cell . . . at a machine or desk, in a mill or mine where even a job can seem punishment . . . in a divorce court or the purgatory of a loveless marriage . . . in the cruel tearings of family conflict—there are new people being born. Coming forth stronger and finer. Seeing themselves, perhaps for the first time, in all their reality and true potential.

"The best years of your life may be the

years of your failure, your heartbreak, your loneliness," wrote Air Force Chaplain Thomas E. Myers before his own death in a crash with his men. "When you discover *why* you have life and go one step further, decide that no matter what cost may be involved, you will follow that *why* until you see yourself the 'man God meant.' ... You will have found that special thing which the God who made you planned for only you to build, to create, to cause to grow."

That may be one "reason" for suffering. Never God-caused but forever God-used, if we but have the courage to turn to that source implanted within us.

FOR EVERY CROSS I'VE CARRIED

Thank you, God, for every cross I have ever had to carry. For every burden I have ever had to bear. For every honest tear I have ever shed.

Thank you for my troubles—they give me courage.

Thank you for my afflictions—they teach me compassion.

Thank you for my disappointments— through them I learn humility and am inspired to try harder again.

Thank you that in fashioning this world you didn't see fit to spare us from the evil you knew would be there. Thank you for not keeping us like dumb animals in a corral. That, instead, you freed us, gave us the dignity of making our own decisions, even if it also meant we must stumble and fall and suffer in order to rise again.

Thank you that in every aspect of our lives you are always near us. Loving, protecting, helping. Hearing our prayers and giving us the strength to endure what we must for our own souls' growth.

I know you, Lord, in times of peace and plenty. But when life is easy it's too easy to forget you; I don't need you quite so much. When life is tough, however, when I see nothing about me but trouble and torment, then I must find you, I must have you! I go crying to you through the darkness,

knowing that though the whole world for-
sake me you will not turn away.
My very suffering brings you near.

LETTER FROM BARBARA

Two of the chapters included in this book
("Pain" and "Death"), first appeared in
How Can I Find You, God? Shortly after
that book was published I received the following letter. One of the most eloquent and
moving I have ever read. I feel this woman's
testimony must be shared, not because I had
anything to do with it, but solely in the
hope her remarkable release will help
others.

Dear Marjorie,
   May I call you by your first name? I feel
like we are friends, even though I haven't
finished your book. I am so overwhelmed
by what you have to say that I am being
compelled to write you at three o'clock in
the morning. I have prayed for guidance;
please put all else aside and listen to me. (I

44

assure you I have never done anything like this before.)

To begin—I got along just fine with you up to page 18, your chapter called "Birth." It hurt me terribly; I was angry and bitter, because you see I cannot have children. My two sons are adopted. "How dare she infer that only a woman who gives birth is blessed?" (I am sharing these thoughts with you, not as a criticism, but as a witness to how God's love can work a reversal of the soul. I had not yet seen the light, not released these grievous harborings, because I had not yet realized that's what they were!) I love my boys fiercely, as much as any woman who ever carried a child. . . .

But I overcame my resentment and pushed on. Now comes the deeper part. Not my story, and yet it must somehow become my witness to God's great love for each and every human being, no matter what the circumstances. Of course, as you say, God doesn't "allow" terrible catastrophes; they just *are!* Pain is not God's will, God's way, only a fact of life. It is what you do with the pain, with the fact of life and death that is important.

All right, let us say I am still reading your book. I am starting on page 149, "Pain." Thoughts are racing; thoughts like, "You've been pretty terrific so far, but my dear you are not going to tell me a thing about pain. Or death. You see, *my pain has been the death of my loved ones . . .*"

Then, in that chapter on pain, I read: "For every cross I've carried, thank you, God. For every burden I have ever had to bear. For every honest tear I have ever shed . . ." And the rest. Suddenly, overwhelmingly, I realize that *I do not want to give up my pain!* After all, I have had to be a martyr to that pain; my whole family has. Dear Lord! Not everyone suffers the loss of five loved ones, in less than a month!

It began with the fire. My twenty-nine-year-old sister, nearly six months pregnant. (The perfect baby girl was left within her womb. I cannot bear a child; why *her* and not me?) Her two healthy, bright, wonderful daughters, ages six and eight. They weren't only her daughters, they were mine too, in the event anything ever happened to her. Mine because they were the daughters I never had. Mine because I helped raise them during a time all three of them went through living hell. Her husband, the girls' father, was a terrible man; they suffered much before the decision was made to leave him.

How could I release this to the Lord? My family and I paid for this pain ourselves, in agony. And a week after their death, more to come! Bette's husband, the girls' new father who loved them, who was in the process of adopting them. There had been hope for him. He had been badly injured, but was out of the coma. He could sit up, consume some food, communicate even though he had a "trach" tube in his throat. And he had to be told they were gone. We were with him when he printed the word "Wife?" with his fingers. The doctors had decided to tell him the truth.

This great young man, who had shown my sister and her girls what the love of a husband and father was all about, experiencing the pain, literally, of fire and hell and such loss—finally to have his own life taken when it had seemed so sure he would survive. *I must give up this pain too?*

And then, only a week later, my father. *Gone.* Heart attack, my eye! He died of a broken heart.

I wanted to fling your stupid book across the room. Again the words lunged at me, "Thank you, God, for every cross I have ever had to carry . . ." My God, my God, I cannot thank you for this pain! If I thank you for it, then I must release it to you, and this I cannot do! To survive, I must keep it and hug it to me. It is mine! *I paid for it!*

I am by myself still. Again, the Lord's way, for I needed complete solitude for the decision I was about to make. I paced the room, your book in my hand. I went to the kitchen cupboard, laid your book on it, and read aloud again: "Thank you, God, for every cross I have ever had to carry. For every burden I have ever had to bear. For every honest tear I have ever shed." No, Lord, I cannot. But I must. And I did. *I actually did!* I released the whole mess to the Father, the Heavenly Father. Because I was paying for the pain all in vain. *Christ had already done it for me.* How could I not have understood that before? God forgive me.

I knew and loved these people; they loved me. Would I *rather not have known them at all?* Oh, God, of course not! My last living memory of Sherry, the youngest, is running down the hall to me with her arms outstretched, shouting, just because she felt like it, "Auntie Barbie, I love you, I love you!" The tears are streaming down my face as I write this. But for the first time in four years, they are tears of joy and acceptance.

It is nearly morning now. I can hardly wait for the day to begin, for the church to open. The people who attend are my friends. They know of my anguish and have shared it with me. Now they must know of my release. I have never personally witnessed before. But I feel earnestly I now have something to share with many. No more tears of self-pity, only tears of joy for the love of God. *If I can accept this, I can accept whatever comes. Whenever it comes.*

So you see, this is not exactly my story. It is a story of family, of love, of pain, of loss and unbearable grief, and finally with

God's help, joy. I know I want to serve God more from now on. Whether it be witnessing for him, or urging people to cherish life while they have it, or just sharing with a friend, as I have done with you. I don't really know, but I will find out.

Somehow, through all this, I have also released to God the fact that I will never bear a child. Have released all my ill harborings against my sister's first husband (which is a miracle in itself). All the old grudges are just gone.

God love you; I love you; I thank you.
Your friend in the Lord,
Barbara J. F.

II

"Gone Where"

*Yea, though I walk through
the valley of the shadow of death,
I will fear no evil: for thou art
with me; thy rod and thy staff
they comfort me.*

Psalm 23:4

GONE WHERE?

And now—death.

Doors close, and a visible life disappears.
I no longer see that image except in memory.

Has he taken God with him? Have I then
lost God?

When someone dies, we say, "He's gone."

It is a hot night in a little Iowa town. . . .
Footsteps on the walk beyond the window, a
mysterious knocking at the door. . . . My
father rises, I hear the murmur of voices.
The door slams, footsteps are running. . . .
I lie heart pounding, puzzled, filled with
foreboding.

At last footsteps return, more slowly. I
hear the door open, and my father's voice in
the bedroom, saying, oh so gently to my
mother: "Dear, your father's gone."

"Gone!" Her awful cry of disbelief . . . the
shock of her moaning.

I lie trying to comprehend it. . . . *Gone*
is a difficult word for anyone, let alone

a child. . . . To vanish, be no more—inconceivable. . . . *Gone. All gone . . .*

But then a simple resolution presents itself, in the form of a question: "Gone where?" Gone usually meant you went someplace. My father was a traveling man, gone lots of times on the road. He came back; he always came home.

And so I remember hopping out of bed and running barefoot to reassure her. "Don't worry, he'll be back."

"No, he won't, honey, Grandpa's *gone!*"

"Gone where?"

And she held me and rocked me as she wept, she told me Grandpa had gone to heaven. But it didn't seem to comfort either of us. . . . *Gone* in death meant the trip from which there is no return. I would never see my adored Grandpa Griffith again, not on this earth, and I began to whimper, not because I really sorrowed yet, simply because I could not believe it. . . .

Now I realize the validity of that child's question: "Gone where?" For if we believe the promises of Jesus, we do go somewhere.

We, who are God's dearest creation, cannot simply be stamped out, canceled, obliterated. We are not sticks or leaves to be consumed in the fire, clouds to vanish in the wind; we are so much more than bodies, we are miracles of mind, emotion, spirit! It is this that distinguishes us from all else on the face of the earth, animate or inanimate. We are God's children, his companions, angels (fallen angels, yes, but still his angels).

When one of us leaves the earth, it is for another destination. As surely as if he had climbed on a train that becomes just a plaintive wail in the distance, or a plane that dwindles to a speck in the sky. The rest of us can no longer see the plane or train or bus or car, or its occupant. But we know it is taking him somewhere.

"All aboooard! Let's go!" . . . Whether we are prepared for that summons or not, we all know it's coming—to us and everyone we love. And its very inevitablity bespeaks a God firmly in charge. When our time on earth is up (whatever the circumstance, even time foreshortened), God wants us back. He has other plans for us. And no matter how smart we think we are, how independent, how accomplished . . . no matter about our books, speeches, inventions, musical compositions, cures . . . no man or woman is able to say, "Sorry, not me, forget it."

When death says, "Let's go," you *go.*

Good-bys are always hard. Separations always hurt—whether short or long or final. . . . The vacancy, the emptiness, the loneliness, the longing . . . But it helps, how it helps to know that the one we miss so acutely has not ceased to exist, but simply lives in a place where we can't join him yet.

DAD'S ROSES

Death can be a bridge that leads the living to God as well as it leads those who have left us.

Our love wants to follow, our love refuses to let go.

Our hearts go crying after the dear ones. . . . "Wait for me, wait for me!" . . . But they can't, they must continue on their journey and we know we can't follow, not yet. We can only look up, earthbound.

And yet we sometimes feel their presence so powerfully there is no mistaking it. And with it, the presence of God.

For a long time during the first year after my father died, I was aware of him standing among roses, many roses, on a lovely slope of hill.

He had always loved roses. Those he raised were a source of great pleasure and pride. I can see him yet going out to trim them, wearing a beaten-up old sweat-stained hat that Mother deplored . . . his blunt, work-scarred hands arranging them so gently on the trellis, his ruddy face filled with such pleased affection. Sometimes he'd pause to sniff deeply of their fragrance, then remark to anyone who happened to be near—"Pretty, ain't they?"

Now here he was among the roses, many roses. . . . No, I didn't have a vision, and yet the lovely picture would come to me. He was always smiling faintly, with the familiar twinkle in his eyes, as if there was something delightful he wanted to say. And I knew without question what it must be: "Pretty, ain't they?"

Then he would turn and trudge away.

That was the only sad part of this image. That after it he must go without a backward glance for me.

And yet I did not protest it, for I realized he was in your keeping, God. You had your hand on his shoulder. You would stay close to him and close to me.

This awareness . . . sensation . . . define it as you will, came less frequently after the first hard weeks and ultimately came no more. Yet I remember it vividly, and even the memory gives me reassurance. My bright-eyed dad, always so vitally active, had not only gone, he was still going! Though without haste now, without worry or urgency.

He had time to pause and admire the flowers. Time to console me by sharing the wonder. To marvel in his old way—"Pretty, ain't they?"

MOTHER'S BIBLE

Death can also bridge the estrangements between people.

For twelve years my mother lived on alone in their little house with its roses. . . . Then one day when she was eighty-four . . . one bright day after serving lunch for my two brothers who often popped in for a bite and one of their lively debates on how best to improve the world . . . she hung her apron behind the door and went to join God and Dad.

I wish this were quite as idyllic as it sounds. She had not been feeling well for weeks and I'm sure she sensed that she was going. She had made quite a few little preparations, including leaving instructions, written in her familiar tiny script, in the Bible she always used, on her dresser where we'd be sure to find them.

But one thing uppermost on her mind she had been able to do little about. There had been a feud in the family. One of those agonizing conflicts between grown children that tear a parent apart. She had wept over it, prayed over it, but the wounds were far from healed.

But now that the house was silent and we all came rushing back, everybody forgot. People ran sobbing into each other's arms. And there was so much to be done. There was simply no time for hostilities. . . . Yet they refused to vanish altogether even in the face of death. Though proprieties were maintained, even an extra show of courtesy, after that first surge of emotion you could feel them quivering, threatening.

Then, that second night, we saw her Bible on the coffee table.

Not the "new" one given her on some anniversary years ago to replace the heavy, cumbersome old one with its family records. We had already consulted the "new" one. This was the old one so long ago relegated to the top shelf of the bookcase. Yet here it lay, on a table that had been cleared and dusted several times! Who had gotten it down? . . . Mystified, we consulted each other.

No one else had been here, at least no one who would have known or cared about that particular Bible. Yet none of us had done so, and each of us was as puzzled as the rest. . . . That Bible simply appeared; there is no other explanation for it.

Without a word everyone sat down while my sister opened the book at its marker. It opened to the thirteenth chapter of John. In a second she began to read aloud:

"'Now before the feast of the Passover,

when Jesus knew that his hour was come that he should depart out of this world unto the Father, having loved his own which were in the world, he loved them unto the end.'"

She paused and looked around. All our eyes were wet. Hers went back to the page. "It goes on to tell the story of how Jesus washed the disciples' feet," she said. "And there's this—this place is marked! 'Little children, yet a little while I am with you. Ye shall seek me: and as I said unto the Jews, Whither I go, ye cannot come; so now I say to you. A new commandment I give unto you, That ye love one another; as I have loved you, that ye also love one another.'"

She couldn't go on. She didn't have to. The two who had been so tragically separated groped out for each other's hands. Then they embraced, holding each other as if never to let go.

The peace they made that night was to last. The bridge of death had become the bridge of love that is also God.

THE MESSAGE

Oh, God, my God, you have taken my mother away and I am numb with shock.

I see her apron still hanging behind the kitchen door. I see her dresses still in the closet, and her dear shoes there upon the floor.

Her house is filled with her presence. The things she so recently used and touched and loved. The pans in the cupboard. The refrigerator still humming and recent with her food. The flowers she had cut still bright in their bowl upon the table.

How quickly you called her, how mercifully. She simply stopped what she was doing and looked up—and you were there.

She was ready. She was always completely ready. Yet she must have known that she was going soon. There were bookmarks in her Bible at these passages:

"Though I speak with the tongues of men and of angels and have not charity . . ."
Surely this was her message to us—to be at peace between ourselves. And:

"When Jesus knew that his hour was come that he should depart out of this world unto the Father, having loved his own, which were in the world, he loved them unto the end."

To the end. She loved us too to the very end.

Help us, who were her children, to draw near to each other now. And near to her. And through her, nearer to you.

FACE TO FACE

I am searching for you, God. I am trying to find you.

Sometimes you are close, as close as my own hand, my own breath. Again you disappear. I get too busy to pray, too busy sometimes even to think.

And though I feel a vague loneliness, unease, it doesn't seem to matter too much. I have all these other people to talk to, warm living people to work for and love and touch.

Then one of them is torn from me. . . . The phone rings. Or an ambulance comes

65

screaming to my steps. . . . A doctor beckons, looking grave . . .

Then I cry out to you, "My God, my God!" . . . Whether in sheer anguish or anger, I call out to you. Then, as never before, I find you.

Death brings us face to face.

When this happens, all those things I have read or been told—how easy they are to forget. This is not somebody else's concept or philosophy of death. This is *my* death. My flesh-and-blood death to deal with. And now, as at no other time, I must decide whether or not I want any part of God.

But I must realize: If, in my agony, I turn away from God, then I, too, go down into death. The death of all hopes ever to see the one I love again (for I cannot reject God and still claim his promises). And the death of my own spirit. For life can never again have the meaning it had when both he and my God were in it.

If, as I must say good-by to the one who meant so much to me, I also abandon God, then I am doubly bereft.

If, in my pain, my almost intolerable

66

sense of loss, (I blame God, I am destroying myself. The words in Job, "Curse God, and die," mean exactly that. To curse God *is* to die in the vital core of self.

Have I ever found God? Do I truly know him? Death puts us to the test. And sometimes the closer we think we have been to God, the more severe the test. . . .

I thought you loved me! I prayed, I had such faith—and now this!

I feel sure God understands. For we are only human, bound to those we care about with such fierce hot human ties. It is natural to weep, protest. (Jesus wept, too, at the death of his friend.) And we are like children; all of us are really children inside these grown-up bodies, especially when we lose someone. Like children we lash out at what we can't understand. Then, when the storm has subsided, we must be comforted. We plunge gratefully into the arms of the person we trust.

This is the time for God. Our own Creator. The one who not only gave us life but created and shared with us the life we loved so much. Where else can we turn for any real assurance that that life or our own lives have any meaning? God alone knows the answers, and in God alone can we find them, through his son.

Living in a time of slavery and slaughter, when life was considered cheap, Jesus told us over and over how precious life is. That not one sparrow falls without God's knowing and caring, not one hair of our head is harmed. . . . Living in a hot and arid country, where only the winter rains fill the cisterns or there is a single well for the town, he knew how constantly people were thirsty. Yet he spoke of the deeper thirst, the thirst for God. He told us to drink of the well of living waters, that we might have life everlasting. He told us that our time here is but the flick of an eye compared to eternity, and actually only preparation for the richer life beyond.

We hear those words so often at funeral sermons we forget they were not preached as funeral sermons. Jesus was speaking to people in farms and shops and homes, on busy highways and village streets. Not in hushed chapels with organ music playing and the heavy fragrance of floral wreaths. Not simply to comfort the bereaved. What he was telling those people, and us, was meant as a challenge to a more abundant, generous, God-trusting life here that would lead to an even greater life.

THE LESSON OF LOSS

Thank you, God, for the wonderful lesson of loss.

The arms of my friends console me, the love of my family surrounds me. The goodness and kindness of my neighbors sustain me like a staff.

Though I am prostrate with grief I am supported, as by a great shining column that rises up within me. I can lift up my head, I can walk upright. I can even smile.

For their sympathy is also like a lovely pool in which I see glimpses of goodness and beauty never revealed before. In it my agony is soothed, the ache of my heart becomes bearable and will, I know, one day heal.

Surely if human beings can surround and help and support each other in such times of sorrow, then your love, oh God, must be even more great.

I feel your kind hand upon me through the touch of theirs. I feel your promises fulfilled.

I see my dear one fresh and new and whole, free of pain and problems, spared of all distress. I see that dear one lifted up into some new state so joyful and free and on-going that excitement fills me.

I sense that blessed presence saying, "It is true! It really is. Believe this, oh believe this and don't grieve."

I am enriched by this loss. My faith is renewed. I am a better person for it.

God of our creation, God of our ongoing, thank you for this wonderful lesson of loss.

PROMISES TO KEEP

"The Lord gave, and the Lord hath taken away. . . ."

That familiar quote from Job. Mr. Malone (the minister in our little Christian church at home) used to challenge this. Got

70

almost angry when he heard people speak of God's "taking" someone. "The Lord didn't take that child," he said. "A germ did." "The Lord didn't strike that man. A car did."

We are all subject to natural laws. When something goes wrong, when a law is broken, disaster follows. . . . But God is the author of the universe, source of those natural laws. Can't he change things to please us? What about miracles? What about prayers?

It is all such a mystery; we study and speak and search and discuss and know so little. Erudite as we try to sound, we know, actually know so little.

That's got to be where faith comes in. . . . Do we ever need faith quite so much as when a life is snapped off unexpectedly? Suddenly, shockingly, one day here, the next day gone. A young life, especially, so full of joy and promise . . . faith, no matter what. The deep wordless recognition that what *is* must be accepted and does not mean God has abandoned us, nor intentionally done that young life in. . . . But God's *will?* No, I don't think we'd better get faith fouled up with God's will. . . .

That little girl rushing home from school eager to show her mother her drawing and a report card full of A's. . . . How can I believe in a God who would decide: "Aha, I shall cheat that mother of even that brief happiness, I won't even let her reach the doorstep, I'll take that child right now!"

Or my friends Frank and Sara Foster, en route to a Baptist convention with another ministerial couple, Joe and Diane Wortman. Beautiful parents with two children apiece; both had built flourishing churches; they'd witnessed in the streets and were planning a camp for homeless boys. . . . So much accomplished already, so rich a harvest ahead. . . . "The convention is waiting for them; Sara is supposed to sing (I gave her the voice of an angel). Nobody doubts they'll get there, but I've got other plans for them. I'll send a storm to bring that small plane down. . . ."

No, I don't even want to find a God like that. Any god worthy of my worship at least has common sense. And my God is a god of mercy, of fair play and compassion as well as a god of power (who can and continually does work miracles and answers prayers).

72

My God would never deliberately bring harm to anyone. But if it happens—if it simply happens due to wind and rain and weather and man's own mistakes, then God has promises to keep:

Life continuing. An even richer, fuller, brighter ongoing life to compensate.

Lord, dear Lord, I will hold fast to you and remember:

You did not take those young lives, but you received them. (How gently and how generously you received them!)

You did not will their going, but you accept their return.

You did not cut short their time of growth and happiness on earth, but you will enhance and enrich their time of growth and happiness where they have gone.

I will not grieve for what they have lost, I will rejoice for what they have gained.

I will not blame you for what happened; but I will thank you for what is happening now. To them, as they know you in person. To me, as I know you in spirit.

Thank you that your love can turn tragedy into triumph.

SO SHORT, BUT OH SO SWEET

And I must remember this about the death of the young. Sometimes a mission on earth can be accomplished in a very few years. (Jesus didn't live very long either.) Isn't it possible that the work someone may have been sent to do is finished?

Not in the case of those young ministers. No, no, that seems senseless; they were all set to help so many more, to do so much more *good*. But others? At least some others?

One thing is certain: A short life can be an intensely sweet one; almost always sweeter and purer than a life prolonged. Any parent who has lost a child acknowledges this. You sorrow for the joys of life that child has missed, but you recognize the pain and problems it has been spared. It goes back to its maker unembittered, unscarred, leaving only the most beautiful memories behind.

And we know—every instinct knows with some deep knowledge—that life does not stop, whatever its stage of interruption; it continues to develop in perfection. And

74

usually far happier than it could possibly be in this precious but battle-wracked existence.

Quite a body of evidence is accumulating about the life experience beyond. Repeatedly, people who have been close to death, or who have actually died according to medical tests, who remember actually crossing over before being brought back by modern scientific technics, such people insist they experienced such joy, such unimaginable peace and transport that they didn't want to return.

HE WAS SO YOUNG

He was so young, God.

So young and strong and filled with promise. So vital, so radiant, giving so much joy wherever he went.

He was so brilliant. On this one boy you lavished so many talents that could have enriched your world. He had already received so many honors, and there were so many honors to come.

75

Why, then? In our agony we ask. Why him?

Why not someone less gifted? Someone less good? Some hop-head, rioter, thief, brute, hood?

Yet we know, even as we demand what seems to us a rational answer, that we are only intensifying our grief. Plunging deeper into the blind and witless place where all hope is gone. A dark lost place where our own gifts will be blunted and ruin replace the goodness he brought and wished for us.

Instead, let us thank you for the marvel that this boy was. That we can say good-by to him without shame or regret, rejoicing in the blessed years he was given to us. Knowing that his bright young life, his many gifts, have not truly been stilled or wasted, only lifted to a higher level where the rest of us can't follow yet.

Separation? Yes. Loss? Never.

For his spirit will be with us always. And when we meet him again we will be even more proud.

Thank you for this answer, God.

THE PROCESSION

The more people I lose to death, the nearer to God I am. I had not realized this until recently, and yet it's true.

When I was young, death was a terrifying stranger who snatched one of my playmates one night. I wept wildly and strove to join him by climbing as high as I dared in the maple tree.

Later, impossibly, the town lifeguard and hero drowned, and we were all in a state of shock; but it was mass emotion and unreal. Our grandparents died, but that was the way of the old. Our parents frequently mourned for friends and relatives and went to funerals, but what had that to do with us, the young? For we were, of course, immortal. . . . And yet, in the haunted catacombs of our souls he lurked, that threatening stranger. "No, no, he dare not touch us, we were too young, we hadn't lived yet, and besides we would live forever!"

Then Tommy crashed. My aviator cousin with his grand helmet and goggles, who was going to teach me to fly. And I knew then it

77

wasn't the old and tired and life-used that death relished and stalked, it was the young. And I was horrified and frightened. It was all wrong and cruel, it had nothing to do with God.

But death becomes less of a stranger as we grow older. No less cruel when we have to give up someone we love. But a force we can accept. Now we are the ones attending the funerals while our immortal young run free. We have learned how to say good-by to people, so many people, and go on from where we were. (Sometimes straight from their services to a party.) Besides, death has been all doctored up now, as if you're not supposed to notice. People don't carry on the way they used to, at least where they can be seen; sometimes they don't even have funerals. It's more as if the one who's died has just moved away.

Yet if you care . . . if you truly care.

The pain that seems at times beyond bearing. The aching vacancy that begs somehow to be filled. Speak of him, oh speak of him—reminisce about him with others, talk about the good times, laugh so you won't cry. . . . And this is good for a while; it helps to be with people who knew him, who can share the memories. But watch out lest you try to make their company a substitute for the one who can't return. No other living person and no amount of talk can recreate him for you. So let go of them, let go as quickly as you can.

And the letters, the pictures, the garments hanging mute in the closet. The records you listened to together, the little jokes and souvenirs. What of these? What of these? . . . Let go. Gradually, little by little, let go; for we must stop reaching backward toward the places our dear ones have left before we can reach out and upward toward the place where they are. Stop hugging them to your breast in grief. Open your arms to embrace them in prayer.

Back in those days when I was so young I remember a minister's saying we ought to pray for the departed. I couldn't imagine why. They'd lived and died, for them it was all over, I thought, their fate was sealed. How could they possibly need or want my prayers?

But when you are older and have lost someone, you don't have to ask. You find yourself praying, not so much for them as for yourself, because it seems the only way to make contact. . . . "Oh, Cindy—" . . . "Oh, Mother—" . . . "Oh, John—" . . .

Dear God, let them know I love them and am thinking of them. Please take care of my darlings.

And gradually the tone of the prayer changes—at least it did for me. I found it became less a cry of desperate longing than a prayer of loving release. A message of blessing. A time to remember those I loved and to rejoice that they were safely in God's gardens. Like my dad.

You get used to anything, even intense personal loss. And you get used to the more and more frequent departures. This relative. That. A close friend. Another friend. A neighbor, a beloved teacher, your boss. . . . You even get used to receiving that first shock. *No.* I can't believe it—not him! . . . There seems no rhyme or reason so often, no special order, only that there are always more. And more.

Until after a while it dawns on you how many there are. It must be getting crowded in heaven! When you try to remember them in prayer, you have to call the roll. But there is something actually joyful in the thought. . . . They are not alone up there. They have "the blessed company of heaven."

And quietly, steadily, all unseen, this procession of departures has been leading you closer to God.

At least so it was with me. With everyone who leaves, I am being drawn, without knowing it, just a little nearer to the original source who designed their destination. And my own.

For as surely as he sent me to this earth, he has given me a return ticket. I know that one day I, too, will be in that same procession. I will join them. . . . And the mere fact that I call their names in prayer, lifting them up, asking for them peace and joy and all of God's blessings, confirms the fact that they are *there*. As I, too, will one day be there.

And so I don't fear death any more, or doubt God any more.

Death has helped me to find him.

THE NEW DIMENSION OF LOVE

I know that they live again, that they live again, my dear ones whom I no longer can see.

You have not taken them into a kingdom—they wouldn't be happy in a kingdom—but you have opened wide for them a place of joy and peace and challenge, where their dreams can be fulfilled.

And this place somehow includes my own small portion of the world. They have not really left me, my dear ones, they are close by me in a way they could never be before.

They know how much I miss them, they know how much I love them. They understand about all the things I meant to do for them and didn't, the words I failed to say.

They put their arms around me to comfort me. They tell me, "It's all right, human love is faulty but for all its faults enduring. It goes beyond such things, it goes beyond even this spearation. The loss of the body does not mean the loss of that love. There is a new life in which that love is even stronger. For God is love, remember. God is truly love."

And this I know. This, God, I know: They are with you now—forever. And so with me forever—in this new dimension of love.

"WE'LL COME"

It seems such a pity that the scattered members of families almost never get together except in times of loss.

Someone dies. Someone dearly beloved. And suddenly the telegrams and letters begin to fly, the phone calls are being made. People who correspond only at Christmas now send wires, special deliveries. People who haven't heard each other's voices in months, even years, are communicating: "Oh, no! I'm so sorry—when did it happen? We'll come. We want to come." . . .

We'll come. We want to come. . . . Suddenly it seems imperative. It is a compelling desire. For the news that has summoned us in the cause of sorrow has warm and quite

83

wonderful overtones. We must go, we must draw together in this hour when one of our own has passed. We want to, for the sake of that person, but also for our own. To comfort and support each other. And oh, to see each other again—brothers and sisters long apart. Aunts and uncles and cousins. Yes, and second cousins, too. The whole clan.

So many of them, arriving so unexpectedly from so many places. It is a revelation, sweet and rather startling. Not only that they are so numerous, but that they too should want to come. And that in this busy world where distances are great and relatives tend to become strangers, blood ties still are strong.

How good it is to see them. How consoling. And despite the sadness of the occasion, how pleasant in so many ways. The visits so solemnly begun drift off into laughter and good talk: "I hadn't realized you had so many children. That makes me a great aunt, doesn't it? And they're so pretty—whose side do they take after, ours or Mac's" . . . "Now let's see, whatever became of Lou's girl, Irene?" . . . "Remember the time Dad spanked all of us for going swimming that day the waves were so big?"

Reminiscences. The matching of statistics. News. And the old family friends who are so much a part of the past that they too belong: "Your papa came running to our house the night you were born." ... "Your mother and I went to school together—" The family doctor who saw you all through so many illnesses is there. The neighbors from the old house on Seneca Street.

They too wanted to come. Out of respect to the one who is gone, yes, that is their excuse. But mainly to claim their own memories of the lost days once again, days in which he played a part, the precious days that are past.

And as you all sit around laughing, talking, eating the food the neighbors have brought in, you remark: "How Dad would have enjoyed this. Oh, how happy he would have been to be with all of us." And you add, "If only people could have get-togethers like this when we're all alive!" And everyone agrees.

But we can't. This too we acknowledge. We are so busy, so far apart. It takes the deep seriousness of death to draw us, to make us realize that all lives that relate to us are dear—these scattered lives. And when it is all over, though you rejoice at having claimed them once more, it is sad to say good-by. Then a dear little woman, strong in faith, says simply: "We'll meet again. Don't worry, it's all right. We'll all meet again."

Again something warm and wonderful comes over you. You realize, "Why, yes, that's right. He'll be there too—and we'll all be together again!"

III

When Loneliness Is New

*I call to remembrance my song in the night:
I commune with mine own heart.*

Psalm 77:6

GOD SAYS, "GET UP!"

Again and again God says, "Get up!"

Sometimes he speaks through people, and it seems a harsh, unfeeling physical command. . . . I am ill. Pain-wracked. Anyone can see I'm in no condition to leave my bed. Yet the doctor and the nurses enter, and to my astonishment say, "Let's get you up awhile today. You must get up."

Sometimes it is but the voice of the stern but loving command of the God without and within. . . . I am prostrate with grief, my life is in shambles, there is nothing left for me now but the terrible comfort of my tears. . . . Dimly, beyond drawn shades, I realize the world is going on heartlessly about its business. People pass by, some of them even laughing, outside on the street. . . . The telephone rings. There is a knocking at my door.

I stuff my ears, try to burrow deeper into my awful loss. Then the voice comes strong and clear: "Get up."

91

"I can't, I can't. . . . O God, I can't."

It comes again. This time more imperative than the telephone or the doorbell or the awareness of duties to people who need me. *"Get up!"*

Startled, I stagger to my feet . . . grope protestingly for some means of support—and find it. A chair to lean on, or unexpectedly the arm of a friend. . . . But in a few minutes I realize I won't need them, for there is another support beside me. God has provided the brace. He would not call me back to action otherwise. He will sustain me.

It is so easy to "quench my thirst with tears and so learn to love my sorrows," as the Paulist priest James Carroll wrote. So easy, and often so tempting, to fall in love with our own misfortunes. For that way lies sympathy (if sometimes only self-sympathy) and possible escape. . . .

We're tired, fed up with this rat race, this drudgery; we don't want to work. . . . "Get up. Do it!"

We are ill and nurturing our own illness. . . . "Get up. Get well."

We are stricken with sorrow or shame; our troubles overpower us, we long only to sink into the slough of our despondency behind locked doors. . . . The command rings loud and clear: "You cannot bury yourself any longer. Get up! Get on with living."

Again and again Jesus said those words. To people lying in sickbeds or even on deathbeds: "Arise! Get up." And they did, and were well and lived again. He is saying them still to anyone who will listen: "Don't give in to your pain and problems. Don't nourish your grief. Get up."

Thank you, Lord, for never failing to say them to me.

Life is too short and too sweet to squander in the darkness, crying. Thank God, thank God you always get me up and back into action. This, as nothing else could, proves how much you care for me.

WHEN LONELINESS IS NEW

Loneliness is so new to me, Lord. I need your help in handling it.

93

Help me to be a little more proud. Not aloof, but a little less eager for human contact. Let me remember that other people are busy with their friends and families. Don't let me overwhelm them with invitations.

I don't want them to feel obliged to come, out of concern for me. And certainly under no obligation to "do something for me" in return.

This is a delicate area, Lord—help me to handle it sensibly and cheerfully.

Please guide me too when it comes to accepting invitations.

My loneliness is sometimes so acute I feel I'd go almost anywhere at any time with anybody. This is an affront to my self-respect.

Don't let me be too proud, too choosy, but don't let my desperation show or get me into situations I'd regret.

Lord, help me not to talk too much when I do go out. Especially about myself—my problems, my grief.

Let me remember how I've dreaded seeing other lonely people who pinion friends to hear their tales of woe. Don't let me cheapen my sorrow by wearing it on my sleeve.

Lord, make me such good company that I will still be wanted. Help me to remember that I'm not the first person to face loneliness, and I won't be the last.

Thank you, Lord, for giving me the grace to handle loneliness.

THE LONELY WOMEN

God bless lonely women.

All lonely women who come home at night to find no man there.

No scent of smoke lingering. No ashtrays overflowing. No exasperation of men's dear strewings—socks, papers, coins, keys. No sweet tang of shaving lotion and cigars.

God bless all lonely women who will not leap at the sound of a strong male step on the stairs.

God bless women, all the lonely women who lie mateless in the night, hungry for the comfort of arms around them. A strong

95

shoulder to rest on (and cry on and complain on). A male presence to depend on, sensible or brave when threatening noises pierce the dark.

God bless women without men to solve things, fix things, find things—bills and problems and toasters and washing machines and missing fuses so there will be light.

Women who have no man to zip them up, repair an earring, run an errand, share a hope, a dream, a memory, a surprise.

God be gentle with women who have loved men, lost men, or missed the marvel of being with men.

And put gentleness in the hearts of all women who still have men—that they may be kinder to the lonely women, and infinitely more kind to the men who share their lives.

SHE SITS IN DARKNESS

I thought I was lonely, Lord, until I found this woman.

She is blind, quite blind; she sits alone in the darkness.

She is deaf, quite deaf; she sits alone in the silence.

She is ill, quite ill; it is difficult for her to move.

I cannot speak to her, I cannot let her know who I am. I can only press her hand and try to comfort her by my presence, so that she will not feel quite so alone.

Lord, I know now what loneliness is. I have been in its presence. I know that I am not truly lonely, after all.

I can see—I have the company of magazines and books.

I can hear—I have the company of my radio, my telephone, my TV set.

I can move, Lord. I can go about my work, my errands, and go to call on this woman.

"Who am I?" I have often asked of you, and of myself. How much more this question must torment anyone lost in the silent darkness.

I must help her to find an answer to that question. I must let her know, somehow,

that she is real and important. Very impor-
tant. Very real.

She has deeply touched another human
being. And because of her I am less lonely
and less lost!

God, convey this to her. Help me to make
her aware of this.

THE LOVELY SOLITUDE

I've just come from visiting a big noisy
family and I'm exhausted. Filled with happy
memories yes, but glad to get home.

And now seems a good time to realize that
instead of lamenting my loneliness, I should
be singing the blessings of solitude!

Thank you for silence, Lord. Sheer si-
lence can indeed be golden. And so can
order. I gaze about this apartment with new
respect; it seems beautiful right now, and
simple to keep it so with nobody to pick up
after but myself.

And independence—how divine. The
freedom to do what I please.

I can listen to the kind of music I really enjoy or watch the kind of television show. I can read, write, sew, paint or just think without being interrupted.

I can read in bed at night as late as I want without disturbing anybody. I don't have to worry about anybody else's feelings, or have my own unexpectedly hurt. I don't have to argue or pretend to agree when I don't.

I don't have to be bored. I can give a party. I can call up a friend for lunch

And even if all the people I know are busy, I have only to dial a few numbers, travel a few blocks to be in the thick of those who'll welcome me with open arms. My clubs, my church—hospitals, the Y, the Salvation Army.

More places than I can count, where there are always vital, joyous, stimulating people; and people whose loneliness and needs so far surpass mine that I feel richly endowed and aglow.

Lord, let remember all this when loneliness gets me down.

And let me remember it also when I get

too enamored with solitude. *Don't let me become ingrown and selfish.*

There is so much work to be done and so many people to be helped and enjoyed. Especially for the woman who lives alone.

PSALM FOR DELIVERANCE

I pleaded with God to deliver me from trouble.

My brain was bruised from seeking solutions. My body ached from the effort. My nerves were strung tight; they would break, I knew, something would break if I forced myself to go on.

"Help me," I kept crying to my God. "Give me answers. Deliver me from this torment." But my own voice seemed to despair of such deliverance even as I called.

Then a strange quiet came upon me. A kind of divine indifference. I knew without words or even thoughts that I could only withdraw and wait quietly upon the Lord.

And he did not forsake me.

100

He came in the quiet of the night; he was there in the brilliance of the morning. He touched my senses with hope; he healed my despair. And with the awareness of his presence came the deliverance I sought.

The answers would be provided. Quietly, and in God's own way, they were working even as I waited.

THE RADIANT COMPANY

The Lord has led me into the radiant company of his people. Praise the Lord.

The Lord has given me the fellowship of others on the selfsame journey to find him.

He has given me a spiritual family. He has given me sisters in the dearest sense of the word. He has given me brothers.

We worship together, work together, pray together. And are as richly rewarded in the praying as those we pray for.

I can worship the Lord alone. I can pray alone.

I can know him fully and completely in

total solitude. And this is good. For most of our lives we are alone. Despite the presence of many people, we are alone.

But to pray and worship the Lord with others who earnestly, honestly seek him, is to add new dimensions of strength and joy.

Praise the Lord for this gift of fellowship and friendship. For the miracles of work and happiness and healing that burst like stars and change the course of lives when people come together who truly love the Lord.

IV

When the Heart Is Ready

*Thou shalt show me the path
of life; in thy presence is
the fullness of joy, and at thy
right hand there is pleasure
for evermore*

Psalm 16:11

THE ADVENTURE

Oh, God, I rejoice in the sheer adventure of living.

Just to wake up in the morning and face the bright mystery of the day!

Even though I think I know, I can't possibly know what will happen before it's over. How many times will the telephone ring, bringing me what voices? What news will come in the mail?

Whom will I meet? Whom will I see? What good friend, what exciting stranger? And no matter how familiar the people who share my hours, what will they do or say?

All these people in the wings of my life waiting to make their entrances. Waiting to speak their lines, to engage me in dialogue that will affect each of us in so many ways.

Words of love, anger, argument, merriment, persuasion, praise—an infinite variety of lines unwritten, unrehearsed, full of pain or promise, or the simple small exchanges of everyday.

How wonderful this is, God. How end-lessly intriguing this daily drama of living.

Now a comedy, now a tragedy, but al-ways, always full of expectation. Always a mystery!

LET ME SAY "YES" TO NEW EXPERIENCES

Lord, don't let me be afraid to say "Yes" to new experiences. New places to go, new people to meet, new things to learn. Don't let me be a coward about trying things—new friends or new foods, new books or new music, new inventions, new ideas.

Sure, it's safer and a lot less trouble just to chug along in the same old rut. But that way lies age and stagnation. The young are so willing to try things. And while you didn't design us to stay young forever, if I'd created a world so gloriously full of creatures, places and adventures, I'd be sad to see my chil-dren cowering in corners, refusing to dis-cover its surprises—at least until they had to.

Lord, thank you for helping me overcome sheer laziness and dread:

DREAD OF TRAVEL Half-eager to go, half-miserable before the complexities and problems any trip presents. How much easier not to have to shop, pack, cope with tickets and arrangements. Just to stay home where things are familiar. Yet how grateful I am for having made the effort. My life's store of friendships, knowledge and memories is enriched because of every trip I've taken.

DREAD OF SPORTS, PHYSICAL CHALLENGE Learning to swim and dive and skate, learning to ski and ride and play tennis. The voices that whimper and warn, especially as we get older: "The water's cold," or "You might get hurt," or "Stay here where it's warm and cozy. Who needs this?" Lord, don't let me give up the things I already can do, or give in to the voices that would stop me from at least attempting new ones. The back porch may be more secure, but the fun is in jumping the fences . . .

DREAD OF MEETING NEW PEOPLE Even the friends now so dear to me were once sometimes frightening strangers. Yet you led me to them, Lord, often against my own resistance. And my life would be empty without them.

God, don't ever take away my courage to try things.
Guard me from recklessness and folly, from foolishly sampling something just because it's "in" but that I know is wrong. Yet with that sole exception, keep alive my enthusiasm, my curiosity and daring. Let me say "Yes" to new experiences.

DON'T LET ME STOP GROWING

Don't let me ever stop growing, God. Mentally growing.
This mind you have given me (any mind!) has such marvelous potential. Why should I hobble it to a house, shackle it to a kitchen sink, cuddle down with it behind a coffee clache?

It's tempting, Lord, and all too easy to give up, make excuses, do the most comfortable thing. To settle for small talk, small interests, small horizons. I've seen this happen to so many women, some of my brightest friends. No wonder they're bored, God. Restless and bored . . . and boring.

Don't let this happen to me. Let me learn at least one new thing about something important every day. (Well, at least every other day.) Let no day pass without reading. Keep my mind always open, lively, reaching out for new interests, new knowledge.

Don't let me stop mentally growing.

Keep me always growing, God. Emotionally growing.

Help me outgrow my tears, my sometimes childish tantrums. The periods of self-pity when I tell myself nobody loves me, like I used to as a little girl. Please rescue me whenever I revert: steer me firmly forward into the calm waters of mature behavior. Let me feel the thrill of self-command, the dignity of self-control.

I want to keep emotionally growing.

Help me to keep growing, God, in relation to others.

So many people need me, depend on me, look to me for help, for answers. And I so often feel inadequate, unequal to their demands. Sometimes I even feel impatient and resentful, not wanting to be bothered. (Why should they drain my time and energy?) Forgive me for this feeling, Lord, and fortify my reserves.

Broaden my understanding. Deepen my compassion. Give me more wisdom and joy in sharing when I can.

As a wife, mother or friend, help me to keep growing.

Don't let me ever stop growing, God. Spiritually growing. Drawing ever closer to you, the source of it all: The universe. The world and the life upon it. The people . . . the person . . . myself.

I want to know you better, tune in more truly with the harmonies of all your creation, including the life that is my own.

Thank you for this person that you made in your image, Lord. Don't let me ever stop growing.

MYSELF

Thank you, God, for the dignity and beauty of self.

The precious, innate self. The only thing that can't be taken from us. The only thing we really own.

Not selfishness. Not self-seeking, self-will, self-gain. But the wonder of being, simply being—oneself.

God-created, God-watched, God-known.

Accountable, actually, only to you who made us. Shaped each of us outwardly so much alike, and yet made each of us so different in the vital, secret self.

You, who expect of each of us different things. You alone can go all the way with us. Take the final journey with us, and be there when we arrive. You will ask the final accounting of this self and its mission upon the earth.

In knowing you I need no longer question, "Who am I?"

I know. Insofar as it is possible, I know. Through you I know the true dignity, worth and beauty of my own being. For whatever

my failings, I am a part of you who made
me.

In knowing you, I know myself.

WHEN THE WINDS CRY I
HEAR YOU

Oh God, my God, when the winds cry I hear
you, when the birds call I hear you, when the
sea rushes in it is like the rushing of my
being toward yours.

You are voice of wind and bird and beat of
sea. You are the silent steady pulsing of my
blood.

I would know you better, I would taste
your essence, I would see your face.

Yet these few small senses of mine cannot
do more. You have defined their limits, you
have set them within a framework from
which we can only see and touch and hear
and attempt to know these marvels that you
have made.

But this too is the marvel—that you are
within each of us as well. As we are drawn

toward your greatness we are drawn toward the greatness within ourselves.

We are larger beings, we are greater spirits.

The hunger for you kindles a holy fire that makes us kinder, gentler, surer, stronger— ever seeking, never quite finding, but always keenly aware that you are all about us and within us.

You are here.

V

"Come Home"

He that goes forth weeping,
bearing the seed for sowing,
shall come home with shouts of joy,
bringing his sheaves with him.
Psalm 126:6

AT CHRISTMAS THE HEART GOES HOME

At Christmas all roads lead home.

The filled planes, packed trains, over-flowing buses, all speak eloquently of a single destination: home. Despite the crowding and the crushing, the delays, the confusion, we clutch our bright packages and beam our anticipation. We are like birds driven by an instinct we only faintly under-stand—the hunger to be with our own people.

If we are already snug by our own fireside surrounded by growing children, or await-ing the return of older ones who are away, then the heart takes a side trip. In memory we journey back to the Christmases of long ago. Once again we are curled into quivering balls of excitement listening to the myste-rious rustle of tissue paper and the tinkle of untold treasures as parents perform their magic on Christmas Eve. Or we recall the special Christmases that are like little

119

landmarks in the life of a family.

One memory is particularly dear to me—a Christmas during the Great Depression when Dad was out of work and the rest of us were scattered, struggling to get through school or simply to survive. My sister Gwen and her schoolteacher husband, on his first job in another state, were expecting their first baby. My brother Harold, an aspiring actor, was traveling with a road show. I was a senior working my way through a small college five hundred miles away. My boss had offered me fifty dollars—a fortune!— just to keep the office open the two weeks he and his wife would be gone.

"And boy, do I need the money! Mom, I know you'll understand," I wrote.

I wasn't prepared for her brave if wistful reply. The other kids couldn't make it either. Except for my kid brother Barney, she and Dad would be alone. "This house is going to seem empty, but don't worry— we'll be okay."

I did worry, though. Our first Christmas apart! And as the carols drifted up the stairs, as the corridors rang with the laughter and chatter of other girls packing up to leave, my misery deepened.

Then one night when the dorm was almost empty I had a long-distance call. "Gwen!" I gasped. "What's wrong?" (Long-distance usually meant an emergency back in those days.)

"Listen, Leon's got a new generator and we think the old jalopy can make it home. I've wired Harold—if he can meet us halfway, he can ride with us. But don't tell the folks; we want to surprise them. Marj, you've just got to come, too.

"But I haven't got a dime for presents!"

"Neither have we. Cut up a catalog and bring pictures of all the goodies you'd buy if you could—and will someday!"

"I could do that, Gwen. But I just can't leave here now."

When we hung up I reached for the scissor. Furs and perfume. Wristwatches, clothes, cars—how all of us longed to lavish beautiful things on those we loved. Well, at least I could mail mine home—with IOUs.

I was still dreaming over this "wish list" when I was called to the phone again. It was my boss, saying he'd decided to close the office after all. My heart leaped up, for if it wasn't too late to catch a ride as far as Fort Dodge with the girl down the hall! . . . I ran to pound on her door.

They already had a load, she said—but if I was willing to sit on somebody's lap . . . her dad was downstairs waiting. I threw things into a suitcase, then rammed a hand down the torn lining of my coat sleeve so fast it emerged mittened and I had to start over.

It was snowing as we piled into that heater-less car. We drove all night with the side curtains flapping, singing and hugging each other to keep warm. Not minding—how could we? We were going home!

"Marj!" Mother stood at the door clutching her robe about her, silver-black hair spilling down her back, eyes large with alarm, then incredulous joy. "Oh . . . *Marj.*"

I'll never forget those eyes or the feel of her arms around me, so soft and warm after the bitter cold. My feet felt frozen after that all-night drive, but they warmed up as my parents fed me and put me to bed. And when I woke up hours later it was to the jangle of sleigh bells Dad hung on the door each year. And voices. My kid brother shouting,

"Harold! Gwen!" The clamor of astonished greetings, the laughter, the kissing, the questions. And we all gathered around the kitchen table the way we used to, recounting our adventures.

"I had to hitchhike clear to Peoria," my older brother scolded merrily. "Me, the leading man . . ." He lifted an elegant two-toned shoe—with a flapping sole. "In these!"

"But by golly, you got here." Dad's chubby face was beaming. Then suddenly he broke down—Dad, who never cried. "We're together!"

Together. The best present we could give one another, we realized. All of us, just being here in the old house where we'd shared so many Christmases. No gift on our lavish lists, if they could materialize, could equal that.

In most Christmases since that memorable one we've been lucky. During the years our children were growing up there were no separations. Then one year, appallingly, history repeated itself. For valid reasons, not a single faraway child could get home. Worse, my husband had flown to Florida for some vital surgery. A proud, brave man—he was adamant about our not coming with him "Just because it's Christmas," when he'd be back in another week.

Like my mother before me, I still had one lone chick left—Melanie, fourteen. "We'll get along fine," she said, trying to cheer me.

We built a big fire every evening, went to church, wrapped presents, pretended. But the ache in our hearts kept swelling. And, the day before Christmas, we burst into mutual tears. "Mommy, it's just not right for Daddy to be down there alone!"

"I know it." Praying for a miracle, I ran to the telephone. The airlines were hopeless, but there was one roomette available on the last train to Miami. Almost hysterical with relief, we threw things into bags.

And what a Christmas Eve! Excited as conspirators, we cuddled together in that cozy space. Melanie hung a tiny wreath in the window and we settled down to watch the endless pageantry flashing by to the rhythmic clicking song of the rails.

. . . Little villages and city streets—all dancing with lights and decorations and sparkling Christmas trees . . . And cars and snowy countrysides and people—all the people. Each one on his or her special pilgrimage of love and celebration this precious night.

At last we drifted off to sleep. But hours later I awoke to a strange stillness. The train had stopped. And, raising the shade, I peered out on a very small town. Silent, deserted, with only a few lights still burning. And under the bare branches, along a lonely street, a figure was walking. A young man in sailor blues, head bent, hunched under the weight of the seabag on his shoulders. And I thought—home! Poor kid, he's almost home. And I wondered if there was someone still up waiting for him; or if anyone knew he was coming at all. And my heart cried out to him, for he was suddenly my own son—and my own ghost, and the soul of us all— driven, so immutably driven by this annual call, "Come home!"

Home for Christmas. There must be some deep psychological reason why we turn so instinctively toward home at this special time. Perhaps we are acting out the ancient story of a man and a woman and a coming child, plodding along with their donkey toward their destination. It was necessary for Joseph, the earthly father, to go home to be taxed. Each male had to return to the city of his birth.

Birth. The tremendous miracle of birth shines through every step and syllable of the Bible story. The long arduous trip across the mountains of Galilee and Judaea was also the journey of a life toward birth. Mary was already in labor when they arrived in Bethlehem, so near the time of her delivery that in desperation, since the inn was full, her husband settled for a humble stable.

The Child who was born on that first Christmas grew up to be a man. Jesus. He healed many people, taught us many important things. But the message that has left the most lasting impression and given the most hope and comfort is this: that we do have a home to go to, and there will be an ultimate homecoming. A place where we will indeed be reunited with those we love.

Anyway, that's my idea of heaven. A place where Mother is standing in the door, probably bossing Dad the way she used to about the turkey or the tree, and he's enjoying every minute of it. And old friends and neighbors are streaming in and out and the sense of love and joy and celebration will go on forever.

A place where every day will be Christmas, with everybody there together. At home.

"COME HOME"

What is this strange compulsion to go home again? The place you were so anxious to leave, yet can never leave altogether. Too much of you is rooted there. You thought that you were tearing yourself free, bloodily by the roots, yet fragments always remain tenaciously. They are stronger than you think. They tug at you when you go back, they tease and torment you. They people the streets with ghosts, one of them yourself. "This is where you began, where you belong. Come back!" they seem to call.

Yet as Thomas Wolfe said, "You can't go home again." The change is almost too much to bear. And yet the sameness, the sweet tantalizing sameness . . .

When I was home the spring before Mother died we all piled into the car one night after supper and went for a ride. It was sunset, one of those dazzling, burning sunsets that turn the lake into molten gold and stirred me so as a girl. The same docks jutted, the same gulls wheeled, the same droves of little black mudhens were riding, plunging, riding their crests as the same tireless waves foamed in. The lake, mysterious, old, gray-green friend, was rolling in as it has for generations. Grandpa Griffith was chased across it by the wolves one winter. Grandpa and Grandma fished here, Mother and Dad courted in its shady parks. And so did we. Every walk and bench and statue is a silent shout of memories.

But change has disturbed its shores. Manawa Beach, where we used to hike and drink the cold spring water, is now suburbia. Even the farms whose pastures went down to the water have been broken up for handsome new homes. Showplaces all, straight out of magazines. My brother pointed them out: "The Schallers built that place. Next door is Dick Richardson. That's Zene White's—" On and on. He and his

128

wife know them all, and the names they recite are often familiar but just as often strange. "The Hershbergers? Oh, he's the new coach at Buena Vista college. The Dyvads built that one—Harry's on the city council now." My brother and his wife never left our little town, and its occupants and alterations are as familiar to them as the doings of their own family.

There are other changes more staggering. Gone is Curt Bethard's huge old weather-scarred boathouse where we learned to swim and hung around all summer, savage-brown, always in love, waiting for life to happen. Now a cement hole in the ground attracts the kids instead. You hear them laughing and shouting, catch a whiff of chlorine from the pool, and feel a kind of affront for the fishy old lake still bashing bravely in. (What's the matter with kids today? We were never daunted by its mighty muscles, we loved its cold embrace. Even on the roughest days or when it was paint-green we went in!)

But branching up from the parks in all directions are many of the selfsame houses on the selfsame streets. There is solace in this, and a curious pain. How can they be here exactly as when you passed them on your way to school or played in them as children? Like the lake, they seem timeless, rooted in sameness forever, totally unaware that you have left and spent a lifetime elsewhere. And it seems that if only you would get out and go to them, you too would be the same. Back someplace in time again, safe with vigorous young parents who loved you, and your heart was not yet broken.

As we drove idly up and down it became a sentimental journey, for we began to call out the names of the people who once lived in these houses. "Redenbaughs were on the corner, the Beattys next door, then the Pattees—she was always so pretty—"

"Then the Crowleys," another voice would say, "and across the street the Sheffields. Remember how Gordon Sheffield used to hang around wanting to play with us older kids?" It became a kind of contest to see who could remember first. Up and down the streets we cruised, piecing the past together through these names. Sometimes arguing, "No, the Roops *didn't* live there, it was the Ringenbergs. I oughta

130

know, it's where I broke my arm when their bagswing broke."

Laughter, a merry uniting of memories along with that dull ache . . . Our pilgrimage draws us even farther into the past. There stands the house where my parents were married. There, even, the small white cottage behind a hedge "where Dad and I met," Mother says. "At a church party. I'd come with another boy, but he walked me home."

Incredible! It mustn't be there any more in its prim white dignity, looking as it must have looked that night. For now, impossibly, one parent is gone and the other is old and must soon be going. "Come back!" the mute houses are crying. "Nothing is different, nothing is changed. Come home." . . .

A few months later the phone rang: it was the call I'd been expecting, and it said, "Come home."

A hometown puts its arms around you when a parent dies. It gathers you to itself like a child. It feeds and comforts you. People surround you, warm living people, and they too say with their food and flowers and their eyes: "Stay. Oh, don't go away

131

again, stay home." Sometimes they even say it aloud.

Church, the Sunday after the funeral . . . and she wasn't in her usual pew. She wasn't leading the dwindling Bereans (the "old people's class") downstairs clutching their worn Bibles. Mother played the organ for years when we were little; and she taught from the Beginners through Teens, Young Marrieds and finally these chipper but faltering few. "Where do they go when they graduate from your class now?" someone once asked her, and she laughed, "To heaven, I hope!" There were so few of them left to gather in that little classroom with its nostalgic smell of all church basements— coffee, hymnals, crayolas. And they looked so lost without her.

But it was Dick, a boy I grew up with, who put it into words after the sermon: "Come back, Marj. We need you. This is where you belong."

I felt strangled. There had been nothing for me here in years; why now? Why this strange compulsion now? For the temptation, however absurd, was intense, and the rejection violent.

"You don't understand. I couldn't" . . .

We spent days breaking up her home. Boxing up memories, keepsakes, and photographs that we'd probably never look at again but couldn't bear to part with. Dividing things, giving things away, cleaning. I walked across the back yard to throw out some trash. The arbor needed painting but still supported the torrent of red roses Dad had set out years ago and took such pride in. They climbed all over the garage and trailed the ground, greedy with life. They were almost too fragrant in the hot sun, their petals spilling. Great trees still arched the yard as if still waiting for family picnics on the grass, great gatherings of the clan. Mother's bag of clothespins was still hanging on the line.

My sister came out and we maundered about the place, remembering. And I said, "Why is man the only creature to experience this awful tie with his past? Memory is both a blessing and a curse, it hurts to recall the days which are over."

"That's because we remember only the good things about them. Looking back it always seems so much better." Then she said, "But man needs memory. Without memory there wouldn't be any painters or writers—no doctors to help us, no engineers, no architects. Memory is what enables man to survive and progress."

And this is true, but it's more than that. Man is the only creature whose emotions are entangled with his memory. And the anguish of memory is what we probably must pay for its pleasures, or whatever progress we gain from it. Bitter or sweet, we don't want any part of life to be really over; it should always be available, if only through people who have shared it. When they go they take a part of you with them. Even when something goes that has been a part of your life story—even that old wooden boathouse.

But the roots remain. The roots that will forever keep calling you back, begging, *"Come home!"*

VI

Beginning Again

O sing unto the Lord a new song;
for he hath done marvelous things! . . .
                                    Psalm 98:1

BEGINNING AGAIN: A TRUE LOVE STORY

This is a true love story. A story of the miraculous way God brought together two people who needed each other, and turned their tragedy into happiness.

It began, for me, with a phone call one bright February day, and the words from a total stranger: "I love you. You have saved my life!"

I listened. As a writer you learn to listen, sometimes puzzled, always expectant, never shocked. You learn to recognize those whose need is real. This was no kook. The voice, as it went on, was rich and refined. He was a doctor from suburban Pittsburgh, he told me, absolutely devastated by the loss of his wife. Unconsolable, however desperately his family, friends and patients tried. Lonely, wild with grief, suicidal. When, on New Year's night, only a few weeks ago, God put into his hands a little book: *I've Got to Talk to Somebody, God.*

139

"It was at the very bottom of a pile of her things. I read it that night, and it saved my life. I read it over and over. But I never even write to authors, let alone try to contact them," he said. "I had no idea I would ever be talking to you. After all, the book was published years ago; I had no idea where you lived, or if you were even alive." Until yesterday, while visiting his son in Silver Spring, Maryland, on the way to Florida. He didn't remember even packing the book, but incredibly there it was at the very top of his case. And there, for the first time, he read the information on the jacket: The author lived not far away, somewhere in the Washington, D.C., area.

"I knew I *had* to call you," he said. "But trying to track down your number took hours." Finally, and again incredibly, he found himself speaking with a pleasant man who said, "Yes, of course. Her husband was my cousin. He died last year."

"Somehow, I knew before he told me," George said. "If you are still free, I would like to come to see you."

Yes, I was free, I said, pleased and touched; but unfortunately I was leaving on a two weeks' speaking trip. By that time he would be in Florida.

"I'll wait," he insisted. And, unlikely as it seemed at the time, he did. When I returned, the mailbox was stuffed with notes, all postmarked Silver Spring. And when I called, simply because I'd promised, he whooped for joy. The next night, though I suggested we meet somewhere nearer, he drove sixty miles to the lakeside cottage at the end of a bumpy country road, where I didn't think anybody would ever find me.

I gasped when he walked in the door, this handsome six foot man, with his arms full of roses. For suddenly, and quite clearly, a small voice informed me: *"You will marry this man before Christmas."* Preposterous! I am not one of those people who say, "God spoke to me, God told me this or that." I can't honestly remember ever hearing such a voice before. Absurd.

It seemed even less possible as the evening progressed. True, an enchanted evening: all the way to and from the cozy restaurant for dinner he sang to me, in the most beautiful male voice I have ever heard. He was poised and gallant and funny, and for real. He had brought along his little black doctor's bag to prove it—filled with pictures, clippings and other credentials. We talked for hours. Here are some of the things I learned about George that night, and later from his family, his nurses and patients and others who loved him:

George and his wife had that rarity, a perfect marriage. "In fifty years neither of us were ever untrue to each other." From the beginning they agreed their relationship would take precedence over everything else in life. As a young physician he prospered early. Leaving the youngsters with willing grandparents, they vacationed together in Florida two months of every year. A third month was spent with the family at their summer cottage on Lake Erie. In September or October they traveled, generally just together again. But between times, he says, he worked long and hard, making house calls and keeping office hours till after midnight, "to put the kids through college and grad school."

Meanwhile, his wife was not only his sweetheart and companion but housekeeper, secretary, book-keeper, nurse. "She handled everything. I never wrote a check or paid a bill. I didn't even answer the telephone." Keeping their social life at a minimum, they spent fifty beautiful ardent years living only for each other.

Thus, when his wife died suddenly one morning, almost in his arms at their Lake Erie cottage, he went into shock. "My whole world collapsed. I was like a child turned out in a strange city in the dark. I didn't know what to do, how even to dial for help. I just stood there and screamed. Then I grabbed a bottle of sleeping pills. I could not imagine life without her; I had to die too, I couldn't go on." The sounds of his agony so frightened one dog, a poodle, it dived straight through a screen and ran. The other, a big golden Labrador retriever, hurled himself against his master's chest, knocking the pills from his hand. "I owe my life to that dog."

Neighbors came. Sons were summoned. He was taken home. From that day on he was like a zombie, a man literally ill, almost autistic with grief. To keep his sanity, he continued to practice, but gone was his laughter, his wit, his songs. Again and again

I have been told by his nurses, patients, other doctors, "You wouldn't have known it was the same man. Before he was always so merry, always singing. You know that beautiful voice of his? We could hear it the minute he entered the hospital, it cheered up the patients, the whole staff. Now he was silent, absolutely broken, and nobody could reach him. Everybody tried but it was useless, he wouldn't accept invitations, go anyplace. He was losing weight, dying himself and nobody could help."

This was the state George was in that New Year's night he had briefly described to me. Alone in the bedroom they had shared, cursing God and wanting to die, he told me, when for no logical reason a picture, his own picture, standing on a dresser clear across the room, suddenly pitched forward and crashed to the floor. No wind, no bolt of lightning, just that sudden crash. "Curiously, the picture didn't even break, although a little china dog sitting in front of it was shattered."

Shaken, George fell to his knees. "Forgive me, God," he begged. "But oh, help me, *help* me."

It was at this point something urged him to open the door to the closet beside the bed. "A white door, whose panels make the sign of the cross—it was the first time I'd ever noticed." Behind it a huge pile of his wife's things were stored. "Not books, I'd gone through all her books the day before, and never even looked at a title. Just dresses, purses, knitting materials, you name it. But something told me to reach down, clear down under the pile. And what my fingers found and brought out *was* a book— your book with a title that went straight to my heart. A book that told me you had suffered too, a lot of people suffer, but with the help of God they can and must go on."

It helped, he said, it helped. But no words, whether written by strangers or spoken by caring friends, can fill an empty house or bring back the voice and touch of the beloved. Still George knew, if only to please his frantic family, he must make an effort to come out of his personal tomb. He was finally persuaded to accept the repeated invitations of a Florida couple who had been very close. "We'll give a big party for you," they pleaded. "We'll even send your plane ticket."

No, he would drive, he told them. So he started out one day, with an intended overnight stop at the home of his lawyer son in Maryland. Halfway to Silver Spring, however, another incredible thing happened. George found that his car had somehow crossed a high, impossible embankment and was heading down the superhighway in the wrong direction! With two huge trucks bearing down on him. He managed to swerve out of their path and smash into a tree on the embankment. Nobody was hurt, although a wrecker had to be called to free the car.

The experience was so unnerving, however, he yielded to his son's advice not to drive on to Florida for a few days. It was at this point he discovered the book in his luggage. "I knew then that something strange was going on. If you were alive and still lived in the area, I had to find you."

I was deeply moved by his story. But when, hours later that first night, he kissed me and asked me to marry him, I gently but firmly said No. "Not because 'this is so sudden.' You're still in love with your wife, George. And from all the things you've told me, I know I never could be the kind of wife she was to you."

"But I love *you* now! The past is gone, it's all over. Something happened the minute I heard your voice, it was like waking up from a long nightmare. And when I actually saw you—! It's not your book, it's you, the wonderful time we've had together just in these past few hours. We need each other, God himself must have brought us together. Please say you'll at least make an effort to know me."

Patiently I explained how difficult that would be. He was still practicing in Pittsburgh. I was busy researching a new book, while winding up promotion commitments on the one just published. "I'm really not right for you, George. A large part of me will always be married to my career."

He looked so crestfallen I groped about for a gift. Perhaps a copy of my latest, *God and Vitamins*. As a medical doctor he would probably disagree with its major premise, that for most of us vitamin supplements are

147

necessary. But so be it. Signing it, I thought regretfully, "Well, that's that. I'll probably never hear from him again."

The next morning the telephone rang. To my amazement it was George, announcing in a voice charged with excitement, "This is fantastic, I just can't believe it. Your book about vitamins—I stayed up and am about halfway through it and I agree with everything you say! I've been using vitamins with my patients for years! In fact, at Pitt I worked with Dr. King, one of the early pioneers in vitamin C."

Could he come down again to see me? No, I was sorry, I was packing for a trip to Israel. Perhaps when I got back.

But turning away from the phone I remembered hearing somewhere: "There are no coincidences. Only Godincidences." Adding them up, I could not but marvel: The falling of the picture. The finding of the book. The accident that could have been fatal, but instead only kept him from going on to Florida. His finally dialing a number that proved to be that of my husband's cousin. And now this.

"You will marry this man," the voice

spoke again. *"You will marry him before Christmas."*

My own marriage was a different story. Good, but like most, far from perfect. The Great Depression was less kind to engineers and free-lance writers than it was to doctors. During our years of struggle my husband and I encouraged and supported each other, but there was no one with whom to leave our four children for vacations, and no time. It was almost ten years before my husband took even a week away from his work, and many more as chief executive with a large corporation in Washington before he managed a month's vacation, let alone four. He was a wonderful man, successful, generous, admired by everyone. "The best boss we ever had," his people said. But desperately driven, partly to compensate for the time he must spend in hospitals.

He had been cruelly burned with X-ray as a boy. Huge draining ulcers on his back showed up while he was still in college. These had to be dressed every night, and frequently cut out, followed by painful skin grafts. Diabetes and three heart attacks took their toll. Eventually cancer began to ravage his body. The last few years of our forty-eight together were torture for him, and agony for those who could not help him, however desperately we tried. Though the children and I moved heaven and earth to save him, and held his hands to the very end, we could not wish him back.

I missed him and mourned him. But for the first time, almost since our marriage, I felt at peace for him—and for myself. God had blessed me with wonderful health. I still swam, danced, water skied and felt about twenty years old. I still had many things to write. And perhaps, after a period of adjustment, there would still be time for love. "Mother, pray for someone special," my daughter Melanie advised. "That's what I did after I got over my divorce from Rick. Two or three times a day I just asked God to send me somebody special. And along came Haris!" She smiled at her beautiful Greek husband, with whom she was now so happy.

Why not? It had worked for her. So each morning after my shower, or in summer my cold swim; and each night, standing on the balcony at bedtime, I would lift my arms and

150

pray: "Please, God, send me a wonderful man who will love me, and whom I can love."

I wasn't in any hurry, I just felt if this were God's will, it would happen. But the man would have to have certain qualifications if I were ever to consider marrying again. On New Year's night, trying to map out my life a year after my husband's death, I half-whimsically wrote them down. Such a man would have to be: 1. A believer, devout. 2. In good health. 3. Successful professionally. 4. Intelligent, well read. 5. A good talker, but also a good listener. 6. Sexy, ardent. 7. A good dancer. (Not absolutely essential, but why not ask for what you want?)

Six weeks later George called me.

I had forgotten all about the list, however. And it was months before I thought of it again.

Meanwhile, George stormed the gates. He did return and saw me off to Israel. And he met the plane three weeks later, again with his arms full of flowers. A bombardment of letters and phone calls followed, along with gifts and more flowers. Easter week he appeared with his dogs, including Ben, the lab who had saved his life. Into his jeep we piled and drove to Ocean City, Maryland, for a week at his son's. A glorious carefree week of running the dogs on the beach, swimming, dancing. He was a marvelous dancer, a magnificent swimmer—a former lifeguard and captain of the champion Pitt swimming team, I discovered. Also one of the most eloquent and entertaining persons I have ever met. Never had I enjoyed anyone's company so much. And so on Easter Sunday, kneeling together in church, when he squeezed my hand and again asked the crucial question, I could resist no longer.

"Yes, oh, yes!" I whispered. Never mind that here was a man who would never get over his wife (I thought). Never mind that I couldn't balance a checkbook, let alone fill the multiple roles she had for him. What really mattered was that God *had* sent me "a wonderful man who loved me and whom I could love." And did!

Thrilled, we rushed home from church and called his family. "When?" they asked. "June," I heard him reply. "No, no, no!" I rushed onto the scene. I had commitments

152

in Canada this summer, a book to finish, things to settle and dispose of before our lives could be joined. "We can't possibly be married before Christmas."

"*Christmas?*" he gasped. How could we endure being separated again so long? We had to, I insisted. After all, we weren't a couple of kids who couldn't wait. "That's exactly it," he said soberly. "We're *not* kids. We don't have that much time."

I was so adamant, however, he had to yield . . . Daily letters and phone calls. Two weekend visits. Then he was putting me on a plane for Allentown, Pennsylvania, where my granddaughter was dancing in the ballet. He would drive on to Maryland to help celebrate his own granddaughter's birthday. We were in tears at parting, but also cheerful, mature. I was making progress, time was flying. We had so much to look forward to. Keep your sights on Christmas.

This was the mood I was in when I reached my son's house and collapsed, from sheer joyous exhaustion. The week before had been spent in New York doing newspaper interviews and talk shows about *God and Vitamins*. On each I worked in the fact that at seventy I was about to become the bride of a vigorous, swimming, dancing doctor, seventy-one. A man who had himself pioneered in the use of vitamins. How remarkable that seemed, falling asleep. How good God was . . . Then I heard it again, the small voice speaking: *"Don't wait!"*

I smiled, overtired, dismissing it; but it wouldn't be still. *"Don't wait,"* it went on and on, all night it seemed. "Don't wait!"

I heard it again the next morning, dancing in the shower. I know it's foolish to dance in the shower, but I always have, especially when so happy. I thought of Kathy, dancing tonight in the ballet. I thought of George. In sheer exuberance I kicked as high as I could, trying to touch the shower head. Suddenly, I was grabbing space. *"Don't wait!"* the voice reminded, as I skidded across the slippery tub, and crashed against its rim.

For an instant I was too nauseous, shocked and pain-assaulted to think. Yet the voice would not be still. Clutching my chest, I crept downstairs. An ambulance was called, the four fractured ribs were taped. I was given pain killers. Somehow I sat through the beautiful ballet. But pain and those incessant words gave me no peace for the next three days. To my dismay, there was no call from George. I was hurt, bewildered, and for the first time afraid. What if his love were cooling? What if his family were urging him to think it over, advising *him* to wait? I had not fully realized how great was my need for him until then.

Finally, on the third night, the call I had been praying for came. My son Mark explained about the accident and handed the phone to me. I was crying so hard I couldn't speak. "Darling, I'm so sorry!" George said. "I didn't want to bother you, I wanted you to be free to enjoy your family."

"Let's not wait!" was all I could think to say. "You were right. Something tells me we shouldn't wait."

"Thank God! I've been in misery."

He would have come at once; he thought I meant now—or next week. Consulting the calendar a few days later, we chose the Fourth of July. Our honeymoon would start in Canada, where I still had engagements to fill. Meanwhile, six weeks to get ready for the wedding.

With the help of sons and daughters, all was achieved. They even shooed me off for a college class reunion one week before. The ceremony, for family and a few close friends, was to be at six o'clock on the patio beside the lake. The weather had been glorious all summer. But we awoke that morning to a raging rain. "Don't worry," the bridegroom said when he called. "I promise you a beautiful day." The blinding rain was still falling, however, when he and his entourage set forth at four o'clock. There were times when the cars had to stop. Yet he kept confidently praying: "Lord, you parted the Red Sea, I know you can part these clouds for Marjorie. She has worked so hard, please do it for her, not for me." And lo, as they turned down that bumpy country road, the sun broke through!

People were mopping up the chairs, bringing out the flowers. The minister arrived, the music began to play. I wore a pink dress the color of the sunset. And as George and I joined hands to repeat our vows, the most beautiful rainbow I've ever seen arched the sky.

We had returned from our honeymoon, and I was packing up books and papers for the move to Pittsburgh, when I came across that forgotten list. "George, listen, you won't believe this," I gasped, and read him those qualifications. "You fill every single one—and more. I didn't even ask God to also make this man handsome. And a great swimmer, with a sense of humor, and a fantastic voice!"

"Who is this guy?" he grinned. "If I ever meet him, I'll kill him." Then, taking that list of specifications to see, himself, he too exclaimed. For it was dated New Year's Day, 1981. "No, I *don't* believe it. Six months ago, to the very day!" He was gazing at me, incredulous. "About what time was it when you wrote this?"

"Around ten o'clock, as I recall. I'd gotten ready for bed. Why?"

"That's when it happened. When the picture fell—I remember thinking at first it was the clock. When I was in such terrible despair—until something told me to reach into that closet, where I found your book!"

The book that was to bring us together . . .

George went back to his patients and I to

my writing. We are both convinced that the best way to live vital, enthusiastic lives, is to keep on doing the work we love. And no two people on this planet could be happier.

Even so, I must try to answer an important question: Is it possible to take the place of a mate who has been loved so long? No. That place will be separate and sacred forever. What the second husband or wife must realize is that a *new* place has been created. No less thrilling, beautiful and enduring simply because this new door to the heart has been opened later. And the richer and finer the love that has gone before, the greater this second love can be.

Patiently, fervently, George had to convince me of that. "Which would you rather marry—a pauper or a millionaire?" he reasoned. "Love is like a bank account. It builds, draws interest. If a man was poor in love before, he would surely have less of love to give now. The fact that I was always so rich in love only means that now I have a greater store of love to lavish on you."

And again: "See that lake, how its waves are rolling in, how it's sparkling with life? But in the winter it's covered with ice too

158

thick to break. I was like that—frozen, cold and dead. You gave me life! You were the sun, melting everything else away. It was all over—the winter of my soul was over and done. And the past went with it. All that matters is *now*, this wonderful joy you and I have in each other today."

It is a joy beyond anything either of us could have imagined. A bountiful harvest reaped after suffering. A wine that is finer and sweeter with age. Nothing has expressed this better than a beautiful card we received from a dear friend. Citing the miracle of the wine at the Marriage Feast in Cana, it concluded: "May it be said of your love in years to come—'You have kept the best until last.'"

Large Print Inspirational Books
from
Walker

Would you like to be on our
Large Print mailing list?

Please send your
name and address to:

Beth Walker
Walker and Company
720 Fifth Avenue
New York, NY 10019

Among the titles available are:

The Road Less Traveled
M. Scott Peck, M.D.

The Seven Storey Mountain
Thomas Merton

**Three Steps Forward,
Two Steps Back**
Charles R. Swindoll

The True Joy of Positive Living
Norman Vincent Peale

The Genesee Diary
Henri J. M. Nouwen

Reaching Out
Henri J. M. Nouwen

Prayers and Promises for Every Day
The Living Bible with
Corrie ten Boom

The Pursuit of Holiness
Jerry Bridges

A Time for Remembering
Patricia Daniels Cornwell

Apples of Gold
Jo Petty

Prayer and Personal Religion
John B. Coburn

Introducing the Bible
William Barclay

The Master's Men
William Barclay

Gift from the Sea
Anne Morrow Lindbergh

The Practice of the Presence of God
Brother Lawrence

Words to Love By
Mother Teresa

A Grief Observed
C. S. Lewis

Reflections on the Psalms
C. S. Lewis

A Gathering of Hope
Helen Hayes

The Irrational Season
Madeleine L'Engle

Words of Certitude
Pope John Paul II

With Open Hands
Henri J. M. Nouwen

The Power of Positive Thinking
Norman Vincent Peale

**Getting Through the Night:
Finding Your Way After the Loss
of a Loved One**
Eugenia Price

Something Beautiful for God
Malcolm Muggeridge

The Way of the Wolf
Martin Bell

Strength to Love
Martin Luther King, Jr.

The Burden Is Light
Eugenia Price